The Enlightenment Plan

Beat Stress, Anxiety and Depression with CBT, Meditation and Mindfulness.

Phil Tyson Ph.D.

First published in 2015 by Equus Proeliator Ltd, 83 Ducie Street, Manchester, U.K., M1 2JQ.

Copyright © Phil Tyson Ph.D.

All rights reserved. No part of this book may be reprinted or reproduced or utilized in any form or by any electronic, mechanical, or other means, now known or as yet invented including but not restricted to photocopying, printing or recording, or in any information storage or retrieval system, without permission from the publishers.

Use of Appropriate Professional Help Disclaimer.

This book is written to help you beat stress, anxiety and depression through cognitive behavioral therapy (CBT) techniques, mindfulness and meditation. It is not intended, nor should it be used, as a substitute for professional advice and/or therapy when needed. If you are feeling life is not worth living or having suicidal thoughts, you are advised to seek the help of a competent professional straightaway. If you are already under the care of a therapist or doctor you are advised to check if following this program will best serve your needs. If you feel the techniques in this book are unhelpful or bring on worse symptoms you are advised to stop practicing immediately and talk it through with a professional.

Results Disclaimer.

As stipulated by law, we cannot guarantee any outcomes by following the strategies in this book. The publisher and author specifically disclaim any implied warranties of merchantability or fitness for a particular purpose, and it should be stressed, make no guarantees whatsoever that you will achieve any particular result. The outcomes you do receive, however, will be in proportion to your commitment to following through on the strategies, and the amount of time you spend practicing the strategies. The suggestions in the book are the minimum required to get the most from the techniques. The more you practice, the likelihood is the more results you will achieve.

ISBN 978-1-910490-00-6 hardback
ISBN 978-1-910490-01-3 paperback
ISBN 978-1-910490-02-0 e-book

Dedicated to

Norma Little

1948 - 2012

For your love and kindness.

Table of Contents.

Acknowledgements 6

Preface 8

1. Unhappy Mind, Unhappy World 12

2. How Mindfulness and meditation Can Help With Stress, Anxiety and Depression 27

3. Reactive Mind, and its Alternative 42

4. Challenging Negative Reactive Habits of Thought 70

5. The Stress Buster Meditation 77

6. The Mindfulness of Breathing Meditation 93

7. The Loving Kindness Meditation 112

8. Mindfulness 130

9. The Enlightenment Meditation - or 'Just Sitting' 142

10. Going Deeper 148

Further Reading 154

Appendix 156

Acknowledgements.

I would like to thank all my clients, whose suffering, and the work we have done to relieve it, has inspired me to write this book. Now even more people can benefit from what we have discovered together.

I would also like to thank my family and friends who have often been at the rough end of my own dips into insanity. I'm truly sorry.

Finally I would like to thank my colleagues, Catherine Millard, Lynn Mackie, and John Milner for commenting on earlier versions of this book. Any errors, of course, remain my own.

 Abandon what is unskillful. One *can* abandon the unskillful. If it were not possible, I would not ask you to do it. If this abandoning of the unskillful would bring harm and suffering, I would not ask you to abandon it. But as it brings benefit and happiness, therefore I say, abandon what is unskillful.

Cultivate the good. One *can* cultivate the good. If it were not possible, I would not ask you to do it. If this cultivation were to bring harm and suffering, I would not ask you to do it. But as this cultivation brings benefit and happiness, I say, cultivate the good.

The Buddha[1]

---

1. Cited in Salzberg, S. (1995) *Loving-Kindness: The Revolutionary Art of Happiness.* Shambhala Classics. p. 3.

Preface.

We live in a remarkable period in human history. The information revolution has facilitated increasing numbers of us 'waking up' not just politically, but also emotionally and spiritually.

In equal measure there are just as many 'casualties' of modern life, those who are overwhelmed by change, and trapped in cycles of fear, stress and despair. These are people who know there is a more rewarding and peaceful way to live life, but don't know how to start.

It doesn't have to be this way, and this book is my contribution to the alternative.

As a psychotherapist working in Manchester, UK since the early 1990s, I've noticed an increasing interest and commitment to meditation and mindfulness. I used to think, like many people do, that mindfulness and meditation was a bit 'cranky'. But then my world fell apart. I lost my health and my life spiraled out of control. I lost my career, my home, I filed for bankruptcy, and I watched both my father and my partner die slowly with cancer. I became profoundly depressed and medicated my pain with anything the doctors and the drug dealers could supply. I was a broken man.

Having trained and worked as a therapist and discovered my knowledge was insufficient to protect me from despair, I turned my attention to the east, and I immersed myself in their meditation and mindfulness techniques, and the philosophies that underpin them. Finally my knowledge of western psychology grew wings. What I had spent my adult life learning in the university now made perfect sense, but only when viewed from the wisdom of the east.

This book is the culmination of all that knowledge. Here you will find the wisdom I have gained both professionally, helping my clients in my successful psychotherapy practice, and personally, in turning my life around. It draws on my academic understanding of psychology, sociology and psychotherapy. More importantly, it draws on my practical understanding of the philosophy and practices of the east.

This book is not, however, a long polemic. It is an intensely practical book. And I give you just what you need to know, and more importantly, do, to overcome stress, anxiety and depression. In the book I introduce you to those techniques that are both necessary and sufficient to help you wake up from suffering. In fact it culminates in a plan, a week-by-week account of what you need to do to beat your pain.

The first benefit of the book is I strip western psychotherapy down to the core of what is effective.

Essentially all the western approaches to psychotherapy suggest that our mental and emotional problems are fictions. They may be painful fictions, but, western psychology suggests, they are fictions none the less. If you are a worrier, for example, you are caught in the fiction of future possible catastrophes. If you are stressed, you are caught in the fiction of things you feel you must do, and if you are depressed, you are caught in the fiction of your self, the world and your future as being hopeless.

Western psychology's tour-de-force is the technique of 'cognitive restructuring'. This cognitive behavioral therapy (CBT) technique cuts to the chase, and empowers you to spot the fiction of your own unique system of meaning. In this book, I take it further, and draw on a broader conception of meaning making than pure CBT. I draw on the whole of the western psychotherapy tradition. I then give you a tool – The Thinking Form – that will help you to literally change your mind, untwist your thinking, and live in a more peaceful and acceptable world.

The second benefit of this book is I strip eastern philosophy and practices down to the core of what is effective.

The wisdom of the east is the profound realization that the only place you can be happy is right now. Think about it, you have never had tomorrow's happiness today. Yet the modern world encourages us to forever discount today's happiness in favor of a future happiness predicated on more money, less weight, better habits, etc.

All the eastern practices of meditation, mindfulness and yoga point to one thing: living in the present. And for me, this is what I had been missing. The tools of western psychology and psychotherapy multiply in power when they are applied to living in the now. Yet doing so is profoundly challenging. That's why we need to practice.

The third benefit of this book is I package all the skills and knowledge and understanding and practices into a life transforming 10 week plan.

The plan starts off very slowly, with just 5 minutes a day, but then builds exponentially to a deeper and more profound understanding of life itself. Happiness, peace and tranquility become an inevitable consequence of the practices undertaken and the knowledge gained in doing so.

You also get access to all the resources you need to complete the plan successfully, including self-assessment measures to monitor your progress, a progress chart and the tool to untwist your thinking – The Thinking Form. There is even a more intense deep dive training group if you feel you need more personalized support.

I imagine that some of you might be reading this and feeling pretty skeptical. I don't blame you. You don't know me yet, and you may not trust my expertise or motivation. I understand this, and I don't expect you to take me on trust. Rather my invitation is to read the book and start doing the practices and be results driven. Let your faith be driven by the evidence of your experience rather than authority.

I do believe with all my heart, however, that the plan contained in this book can work for you. If I did not believe it, I would not have written it.

Your role is simple: all you have to do is read the book and turn up for the practices.

And this is the big promise of the book. Focus with integrity on these practices and you will inevitably leave your 'problem space' behind, and open up to a new way of being in the world - one characterized by greater peace and wellbeing.

Welcome, to The Enlightenment Plan.

1.
Unhappy Mind, Unhappy World.

I signed the contract placed before me. For the Tenancy Manager it was just another contract, letting another social housing apartment to another tenant. But for me it was different. It represented complete defeat. In fact it was the worst moment of my life.

Depression had pervaded every moment of my being. I had lost so much. My health, my career as an academic psychologist, the home I loved, and recently my father to the ravages of cancer. My partner was fortunately in remission from his brain tumor. I wasn't to know but the remission was to be short lived. Future humiliation was also to come in the form of bankruptcy.

I was barely able to function. I couldn't socialize comfortably due to anxiety and shame, and the relentless, unbearable, debilitating depression robbed me of the capacity for joy, and filled my life with an unspeakable pain. I spent my days lying on the coach staring at the walls. I was tormented by the endless routine of washing dishes even though I had a dishwasher. I simply had no energy to have it fitted.

I wasn't to know at the time, but things were to get even worse.

This is a book about cognitive behavioral therapy (CBT), meditation and mindfulness. It is not a book about spirituality, so you don't need to worry: I am not going to sell you a spiritual philosophy, or something similar. It's not that I've got anything against spiritual philosophy, it's just I want to focus on helping people who are suffering with stress, anxiety and depression by giving them help they can use right now. Talk of God, Brahmin, The Source and similar concepts can just seem so far beyond what is attainable when you are feeling stressed, anxious or depressed. At least that is my experience.

So this is a practical book, a 'how to' book if you like: one aimed at those who are as far from spiritual bliss as one could imagine. It is a book for people suffering from stress, anxiety disorders or depression. It will also be helpful for anybody who is suffering in other ways right now, in whatever forms that suffering may take, but my focus will be on stress, anxiety disorders and depression.

I aim to achieve three things:
1. To show you that it **is** possible to 'wake up' from suffering, and you can do that relatively quickly. You don't necessarily need medication, years of psychotherapy, or even the conditions of your life to change.
2. To show you **how** to 'wake up' from suffering. This is, above all, a practical book, one that anticipates your objections and obstacles.
3. Demonstrate what 'waking up' looks like in practice. As I write I'm also doing the meditation and mindfulness exercises I am writing about. I'm practicing what I preach so you can come to understand what it is like to practice and overcome the

common obstacles to effective practice. Every now and again I'll 'check in' with you and let you know how things are going.

You see I have set up a very specific set of conditions in order to write this book.

First, I booked a two-week vacation. Right now I'm on the North African coast in a sleepy Tunisian village. As I write, the sun is streaming through French windows into my spacious hotel room, and I can look out over the shimmering Mediterranean Sea with ships sailing graciously across the horizon. Most importantly, I am alone, and I aim to have minimal contact with the 'real world' and other people. My cell phone will be switched off most of the time, and I'm intent on avoiding TV and the internet.

I also aim to go for a jog each morning, eat light and healthy food, mainly vegetarian and possibly a little fish. I'm going to drink plenty of water and avoid alcohol and coffee. I'm also going to avoid sexual activity and thoughts.

Most importantly, I'm going to meditate a minimum of three times every day.

I can imagine your objections already. "I can't spare two weeks to indulge in a vacation on my own"; "I don't exercise, so jogging would kill me"; "I couldn't stick to that kind of dietary routine"; "I couldn't go two weeks without sex"; "I need alcohol to keep me calm", etc.

The truth is I'm not sure if I can stick to this routine either. For example I've always hated jogging. I like to keep in shape but jogging has always left me cold. So doing the jogging is going to be a real challenge. That's partly why I chose it. I wanted a physical challenge to complement the intellectual challenge of writing a book.

But here's the deal: it doesn't really matter if I succeed or fail. What is important is that I cut out as many unnecessary distractions as possible, and give myself space and permission to 'wake up' from my stress.

You see, unlike most meditation gurus, I don't claim any superhuman insights. I'm no Eckhart Tolle, Ram Das or Krishnamurti. As you will see in the coming chapters, I have had more than my share of problems. In all likelihood, I'm just like you.

I have, however, beaten stress, anxiety and depression with CBT, meditation and mindfulness, and I'm here to teach you, step by step, how to do this too.

But hold on, didn't I just say I am stressed right now? Well, yes, this is true. I run a busy psychotherapy practice in Manchester, UK, and I've also had some relationship adjustments to make. I also experienced a bereavement recently. My longest held friend of 27 years, Norma, died after a painful fight with cancer. You may have read the dedication to her at the start of this book. Those thoughts were for her.

The short of it is that because I've had a lot on, my meditation practice has been squeezed out … and I've been paying the price for this over the last year. I've been getting irritable with my friends, family and even my clients (not a good idea if you want your clients to keep coming back!).

So, I'm human. And herein lay the first lesson of meditation and mindfulness, **the acceptance of what is**. So in the coming two weeks I might not go jogging every day, I might not stick to my meditation regimen, I might sink a gin and tonic or two, ... so what? The important thing is I have made an appointment with you and myself, and I've made space for meditation and reflection, that's the important thing. Perfection, quite frankly, would just get in the way.

So there simply isn't any point in getting uptight by sticking to rules too rigidly. Whatever I do will be an improvement on the previous few months. It is my intention to cultivate meditation and mindfulness. So if I slip up, at least I will (hopefully) do it with full awareness.

At pains of overstating the point, cultivating a non-judgmental attitude to myself is part of the deal. Meditation and mindfulness require, at least the attempt, of a suspension of judgment.

So my invitation to you is to follow me on my journey of writing this book as I apply the techniques I am writing about. I have no set idea of where I will go, what I will write, or where I will end up.

So after making a good start and writing the first section above, I ran dry. I didn't know what to write next. My mind was full of chatter. I was, quite frankly, starting to confuse and overwhelm myself. So I took a break, I visited the hotel bar for a coffee feeling overwhelmed and demoralized (thinking I should never have come!). While reflecting at the bar I thought this would be a great time to meditate. I returned to my room and started with the first meditation I will teach you, the Stress Buster active progressive muscular relaxation meditation.

What was remarkable was that despite still recovering from a night flight, I came out of the meditation energized, not tired. And I got straight down to work. I didn't need to work anything out. I just 'knew' what I had to do next. Here I am doing it! My confusion had gone, and my mood was lifted. I was no longer stressed.

I don't want to say too much just yet about stress, anxiety and depression and how meditation can help, that's for the next chapter, but I just want to make this one point. I teach mindfulness and meditation to people with mental health problems all the time. The one thing I get regularly is 'I haven't got the time'. There are ways to deal with this, but reflecting on what has just happened to me is a phenomenon I now find happens a lot. **If I can find the time to meditate, I become more focused and efficient, and I save the time I spent meditating many times over.** You can do the same. In fact the more stressed, anxious or depressed you get, the more time you need to find to meditate, not less!

In a way, just now, I 'woke up' a little bit. The chatter of my mind calmed, and I knew what I had to do next. That's the miracle of mindfulness. If you stop trying to control the outcome, you get the most amazing results. In a strange way the universe seems to do the work for me, not the conscious mind.

You can get results like this every day; from the minute you start practicing in fact. So I bet you are eager get started, but before we do, I want you to know something about me and what motivates me to help you right now.

I trained and work as a cognitive behavioral therapist (CBT). I have trained and used other therapeutic modalities too, but I like CBT, and use it with most of my clients to some degree or other. It is also a powerful force in the therapy space, and its success is due, in no small measure, to its commitment to relentlessly researching what is effective.

The central idea of CBT is that it is not the things in themselves that are upsetting, but it is our interpretation that makes them so. For example, at breakfast this morning I caught a young womens eye, and she looked away. I interpreted this as disapproval of my tattoos (I love tattoos by the way, and have lots). Now I had no evidence to suggest she disapproved of my tattoos, she could have been disapproving of anything. In fact I have no evidence that she was really even reacting to me at all. She may just have looked in that particular direction as I looked up and noticed her.

Now I know talking about this in such detail makes me sound a little paranoid, but the fact of the matter is we make these snap judgments all the time. As you will find out when you start meditating, it is in fact impossible to stop making them. They have, however, a profound effect on our mood. Without anything being particularly wrong with the world, if we let our negative automatic thinking run wild, we can quickly end up having a bad day. In fact many of my clients are having bad months, and even bad years, because they have fallen into the habit of believing, and emotionally reacting to, their negative thinking. Thinking which, when rigorously examined, has no basis in reality.

As you are reading this book, I'm assuming you are experiencing stress, anxiety, depression or combinations of all three. My strong suspicion is that you also have these unhelpful spirals of negative thinking. You distress yourself when there is no good reason to be upset. The good news is that meditation and mindfulness is the method *par excellence* for stopping these negative thoughts in their tracks, and revealing them for what they are: empty of any real meaning.

What's more, cognitive behavioral therapists are learning that meditation and mindfulness are essential to good emotional and mental health. In fact I haven't come across a new or developing CBT treatment protocol in years that doesn't incorporate some mindfulness and/or meditation.

But Isn't It The World That's Crazy?

Now I'm going to suggest something that, at first take, sounds like a contradiction of what I have just been saying: we live in a crazy world, and its getting worse! Let me explain.

There is what is sometimes called, the 'Whig interpretation of history'. It is the idea that in the past things were worse, and in the future things will be better, and the history of the human race is the story of how we turned a bad situation into a better situation. I believe the Whig theory of history is false. In fact I think with respect to one specific thing, our mental and emotional wellbeing, we have never had it so bad. The world is crazy, and we can't help but be crazy in response.

The contrast here is with so called 'primitive' or tribal societies. Although there is virtually nowhere now left that isn't profoundly touched by modern industrialized life, we have a vast store of research evidence that allows us to piece together a view of what life was like pre-industrialization.

The first thing to note is that human beings lived within a relatively stable, relatively small group of people. A typical tribal person could easily have known everyone s/he met in her/his life by name. Furthermore s/he would have been able to place that person within an extended kin network. S/he would have not only known that person by name, but s/he would have known why s/he knew her/him. Her/his relationships, in other words, came prepackaged with meaning.

The implications for mental and emotional wellbeing here are enormous. The social world for our tribal person would have been stable, slow changing and secure. His or her place in the world would have seemed pre-ordained, and immovable.

This contrasts with our modern world in which we come into superficial contact every day with literally hundreds of people we will never see again. Just think of all the people we pass in the street, and are forced to ignore, as we go to work. Just think of all the people the TV beams into our lives through news shows and drama. Most of them made up characters in made up worlds. Or the endless number of 'friends' on Facebook who, in reality, we barely know.

Perhaps what is worse, we live in an increasingly atomized society. Even a hundred years ago we could have located ourselves in a stable network of kin relations in an otherwise shifting sea of humanity. Now it is not uncommon for siblings and first cousins to barely know each other. Many of us are brought up into families of only one, and possibly two adults; families that are, furthermore, themselves insecurely attached to the wider society. Our relationships with our neighbors are also becoming more distant.

The implications of this are profound. Emotionally we simply are not connected socially to the world with anything like the degree of stability we need to feel secure. It is unsurprising we feel overwhelmed by the world we face, see it as an anxiety provoking threat, and ultimately retreat from it in stress, anxiety, depression or despair. Such reactions in tribal societies would have been reserved for moments of great upheaval. For us, it comes as standard.

Work, and our relationship to it, would also have been very different in our tribal world. We would have worked primarily in order to eat. As the gifts of nature were bountiful, we would have rarely needed to have worked more than four hours a day. We therefore had a life of relative leisure, one in which we could pursue and deepen our relationship with other people, and the world. Indeed perhaps due to the vast amount of leisure, we would have had plenty of time to experience the world, and marvel in creation. If we had any problems, we had plenty of time to work them out. We would also have had plenty of space to just be.

This contrasts with our modern life, where it is not uncommon to have to work ten hours a day, more if you include commuting, to just provide the basics for life. Indeed, life is hard for most of the world's industrialized (and post industrialized) populations, and we suffer the psychological and physical effects of stress, anxiety and depression as a consequence. At a deep level we know we are slaves to the world, and we deeply resent it. Somehow it should be different.

My point is simple. Far from industrialization bringing progress, it has simply brought despair. As the pace of life gets faster, and the resources we need to sustain life dwindle, we can only assume that despair will deepen. Indeed the speed of change is stressful in itself.

For example IT skills I learnt five years ago that were 'cutting edge' are already out of date. If you stay still you will become irrelevant, and it sometimes seems that you need to run to get ahead. Larger and larger numbers of people simply lack the intellectual ability to compete, and are being left behind in slums of emotional, mental and material poverty.

Yes the world is changing, and it is changing fast. The emotional pressures are huge, and we don't have the social support anymore to help us get through. Indeed society is so atomized and divided now that when we do hang out with our 'friends', we do so having no other relationship with them other than we like to hang out with them. They are our friends by choice rather than embedded in an extended kin/tribal structure. This may seem like a blessing but it's not. It means even our friends are expendable. Because we are not economically and social entwined with our friends, we are free to 'outgrow' them. The social world has become perilously insecure.

How do human beings cope with this insecurity? Well we feel stressed, anxious and depressed. How could we not feel these things? But this is not the end of the matter. We start to employ strategies to cope with these feelings. We multi task, over eat, and take drugs and alcohol and call it 'coping'. We 'act out' our despair in suicide, anger and insanity. We also develop mental tricks to offset the despair: we worry and ruminate, we obsess, and we become overly vigilant to the next source of threat.

The technologies of industrialization that we were told were setting us free have done the opposite: they have enslaved us. No wonder we feel ill. In fact science is starting to discover that virtually all diseases are either caused by stress, or made worse by it. High blood pressure, cancer, arthritis, diabetes, heart disease and Crohns all have unmistakable psychological markers. The medicine we herald as our society's greatest achievement simply takes care of the mess it creates. There has to be another way.

So I hold what appears to be a contradiction. As human beings we distress ourselves by overreacting to, and over interpreting, the world we find ourselves in. As human beings in modern post industrial and industrial societies, we also find ourselves in social and economic conditions that create suffering. Paradoxically, both appear to be true. Yes the world is crazy, but our response to it is crazy too.

There is Another Way.

There is another way. I see the shoots of a new way of being in the world where less is more and staying still is the new moving forward. Humanity is starting to wake up to the problems it has created. We need new solutions. That's why I started writing my blogs, MenandMentalHealth.com, TheRenouncer.com and ScienceOfEnlightenment.com. I've joined the steady stream of psychologists, counselors, psychotherapists, sociologists, ecologists, anthropologists and economists who are looking for a different direction, another way.

What is at the heart of this awakening is the courage to open our eyes and our hearts to the reality of our lives, and the truth of our experience. We have learnt that drugs and alcohol, distraction and facile amusement make our problems worse not better. We have learnt that if we pay attention, deeply, steadily, in the moment, without judgment and without an agenda, but with compassion, we not only resolve our problems more quickly, but, rather like I did earlier in the chapter, the solutions we reach are more creative and life affirming.

Paying attention to our painful experiences in life doesn't make life worse, it makes life better. This basic human wisdom, which is our birthright, is hidden from us by a culture of distraction, spending and consumption. It is time for another way.

So who am I? If you are going to change a few things about your life, I guess you will want to know whom you are following.

You already know I'm a psychotherapist and teach mindfulness and meditation to my clients. What they don't know, for obvious reasons, is my own personal struggle. I'll tell you more in the chapters to come, but right now I want you to imagine me locked up in the back of a police van. The call had gone out 'man with knife' and over 12 of Manchester's finest police officers had turned up in response. In truth I was not a danger to others, I was simply a danger to myself. I was at the end of the road. My life was no longer worth living. The pain was too much to bear. The knife was to end my own life.

In one way it was the worst moment of my life. I had been 'arrested' and taken I knew not where. I was cooped up in the back of a police van under lock and key. Yet inside I felt a sense of great freedom. Elation even. It was as if all the rules I had about how 'someone like me' should behave had become instantly malleable. Nothing mattered, not even being detained. I realized I had been trapped by the idea of who I, and others, thought I should be. I felt an immense opportunity to reinvent myself. Something about me had just died and been cast off. Physically my freedom had never been so curtailed. Yet emotionally I had never been so free. I no longer needed to pretend.

Within weeks I walked into the Manchester Buddhist Centre, and my career in mindfulness and meditation had begun. Within a year I had turned my life around. Within two years I was experiencing the profound meditative insights that would shape and transform my life.

Zen practitioners have a saying, "Zen mind, beginners mind". What it captures is that you are closest to 'waking up' to the truth of your life if you cultivate the curiosity of a beginner. If you are a beginner, more's the better. The trouble with meditators is they come to think they 'know' how to do meditation. The problem with this is their expectations of what is, and isn't, a 'good' meditation trap them into a narrative of the possible. A trap as secure as the one they are meditating to escape!

With my 'beginner's mind', I immersed myself in meditation. Without any kind of effort on my part (other than that needed to meditate itself!), my issues seemed to fade away. There was no hard work. It was as if a gentle mist had cleansed me as surely as if I had taken a shower. I transformed and became. Maybe the freedom and release I had discovered in the back of the police van had freed me sufficiently to allow something new to arise, who knows, but I was no longer the driver, I was the driven, and I could see that clearly for the first time in my life. I had learnt that the more I tried to control life, the more life controlled me. Whereas if I surrender to what is, the now, in whatever form that moment may take, the freer I became.

The promise of this book is big and bold: You too can awaken from the suffering of your life and become something bigger. All you have to do is pay attention to your thinking and meditate. Period.

In fact I can also promise you the opposite: if you struggle and wrestle with your stress, anxiety and depression, it will grow. As the famous Swiss psychiatrist and pioneer in therapy Carl Jung once observed, 'what you resist persists'! Herein, of course, lies another paradox about our human nature. My invitation is for you to discover it to be true for yourself. Please join me in the remarkable adventure of mind, which is CBT, meditation and mindfulness.

2.

How Mindfulness and Meditation Can Help With Stress, Anxiety and Depression.

Dave was a client of mine. He was a young professional with a family and was tortured by endless health anxieties. I had been working with him for eighteen sessions over six months and I was starting to despair.

Health anxiety is a diagnosable condition where people endlessly ruminate and worry about illness and death. To help avert disaster people with health anxiety routinely check their bodies for signs of illness and Dave was no different. At least hourly he would check his body for 'lumps' and endlessly search the internet for diagnoses that 'fit' his 'symptoms'.

Cognitive behavioral therapy (CBT) offers an effective way to treat health anxiety, but Dave was not responding well to treatment. As I will encourage you to do in The Enlightenment Plan, I regularly monitored Dave's mood with assessment questionnaires, and they revealed that he was just as anxious and depressed after 18 sessions as he was at the start.

I was frank with Dave. Nothing was working and I told him didn't know what to do next. Then, as an offhand remark, I said

"You are practicing the techniques aren't you?"

CBT is a practical therapy and requires the client to commit to sometimes a lot of homework between sessions. My offhand remark, and perhaps my previous candid assessment of the situation, had left Dave somewhat exposed. As his eyes filled up he admitted

"No, I haven't done any of the homework."

He looked ashamed, and I didn't want to make him feel any worse, but this was the admission I needed. Of course he had made no progress, he hadn't been trying out the skills I was teaching him in his real life.

This situation is not uncommon in my line of work. People want the hour they spend with the therapist to make things right in their life. They actually don't want to change what they think or what they do in their real life. That, actually, is the hard bit.

I guess it is the same with self help books like this one. People want the reading of the book to make the difference, but it can't. It is only the things you do differently in your real life that make the difference. That is why I have broken The Enlightenment Plan down to 10 achievable weeks. If you don't do the plan, the chances of getting the benefits are slim and there is a good reason for this. I will be teaching you new skills, not new understanding. It is the skills that make the difference. Like all skills, to get good and get the benefits you need to practice them to mastery.

Dave wanted the therapy to work without having to do any hard work himself. He was skeptical that any effort he might put in would result in a positive outcome.

My invitation to him was the same as my invitation to you now. Park skepticism for several weeks and give the skills a chance. In this way you will be accepting or rejecting the skills based on good, first hand evidence: the evidence of your experience.

Dave had a go at the skills he had been avoiding, and I'm pleased to say he started to make rapid progress. He was actually quite surprised that after six weeks, when I re-assessed his depression and anxiety, the results showed he was experiencing both with less intensity. This motivated him to keep going.

After several months of consistent progress, Dave hit another plateau. This time his anxiety and depression were approaching normal levels, but he couldn't quite completely shift his health anxiety process. It was then I introduced the idea of meditation and mindfulness.

If I would have suggested this at the start, I'm sure Dave would have walked out of therapy, but at this point in therapy, where Dave had leant to trust my techniques, albeit the hard way, he was prepared to give it a go.

We set about building a meditation and mindfulness practice on the lines of those described here in The Enlightenment Plan. By this time I had taught and perfected the techniques with scores of previous clients. I knew this is what Dave now needed to escape the health anxiety process altogether.

I had such confidence in the techniques because I knew thinking was a little like dominoes lined up for a record-breaking attempt. One domino inevitably falls on the next domino and so on until all the dominoes have fallen. Thinking is a little like this simply because thinking is a habit. One thought inevitably leads to the next and so on. In Dave's case this meant he had himself dead and buried and his children without a father!

The simple way to stop the dominoes is to remove a couple from the line. The dominoes fall until the break then fall silent. Mindfulness and meditation does the same with our thinking. With practice, you become more aware of your thinking processes in real time and then eventually you start to spot the breaks. Once you have done that, it's over for the habit. You simply bat it out of your experience, and do something more useful instead.

This is exactly what Dave discovered he could do. Slowly at first, then increasingly confidently, he was able to notice when his health anxiety thinking process was triggered and found he was able to stop the process in its track. This was just what Dave needed, and I'm pleased to say Dave is still doing well. Of course he still needs to practice, but I'm confident, so long as he does, he will continue to do well.

In Dave's case I introduced meditation and mindfulness at the end of therapy, simply because I didn't think Dave would have been sufficiently motivated to do something so abstract at the start.

For those clients who are open to meditation and mindfulness from the start, I find that it is they who make the most rapid progress. That is why I start The Enlightenment Plan with meditation.

So let's explore in more detail why meditation and mindfulness can help with stress, anxiety and depression.

Stress, Mindfulness and Meditation.

'Stress' derives its name from a mechanical metaphor. If you load something, say a bridge, with too much weight, eventually it shows 'signs of stress', before ultimately collapsing.

When my clients present with 'stress', you can see this analogy makes perfect sense. There are usually two conditions present.

The first condition is that they have too much to do. Life, for my stressed clients, is a long to do list with not enough time to do it in. As a consequence, in order to cope with having too much to do, they tend to over work, and essential life affirming activities like rest, socializing, exercise, healthy eating, and even sleep, get squeezed out. As a short-term strategy this is rarely effective, but as a long-term strategy, it is disastrous.

The second condition is that they believe they have no choice. If you are over worked and believe you have no choice, your only strategy is to keep on working until things eventually improve. My stressed clients think that the harder they work now, the quicker things will improve. This is to sell the current moment in a promise for a better future. Again, as a short-term strategy this can only prevent you from experiencing happiness in the only place you can find it, right now. As a long-term strategy, of course, by offsetting happiness for another day, it can only bring exhaustion. The spiral of stress inevitably deepens: try running at flat out, with a feeling of there being no choice, while you are exhausted: something has to give.

This happened to me in my twenties when I worked as a Lecturer in Psychology at Manchester Metropolitan University in England. Part of me loved the work; I enjoyed writing and delivering the lectures, and enjoyed the feedback I got from students in the process. I was also busy researching and writing my research degrees, and training as a therapist as well! My work life balance was already unsustainable long term, but I was sort of coping. The real trouble came when I was promoted to running a degree program I had been teaching. Suddenly my work life balance disappeared. I remember working 10/12-hour days for a full term with no breaks, not even at weekends. That was over a hundred days straight. I was overworked and trapped and, of course, stressed. I turned to drugs and alcohol to help me cope.

Of course anybody looking in would say the obvious: do less, but I 'couldn't'. My ego was flattered at the promotion, and didn't want to be seen to 'fail', so I couldn't drop 'being' a course leader. My research was why I got into teaching in the first place, that was 'core', and so I couldn't drop that. And my teaching, well if you're a university lecturer, you can't really get away with not doing that. I was trapped by my own and what I perceived were other people's expectations. The way I coped with this, work harder and use drugs and alcohol, gave me a short-term release, but meant when I awoke hung-over the next day, I simply wasn't in a position to do the work efficiently. This, of course, just compounded the feeling of having too much to do, and inevitably, of being stressed.

This tunnel vision is common with my clients who experience stress. They do things the way they do simply because they cannot conceive of doing it any other way. The more stressed they become, the more tunnel visioned they appear to become. Eventually, if something radical is not changed, it is the body that gives way first.

In my case I caught the flu but worked through it. I ignored the fact I was urinating blood, as that didn't fit with my schedule. I only took myself to bed when the pain in my testicle became too overwhelming. I didn't call the doctor, because she would have signed me off work, and I didn't have time for that. So I ended up in hospital in an excruciating pain I hope I will never have to endure again. In trying to save a couple of weeks off work, because of my stressed 'tunnel vision' mind, I had to take two years off instead. My career as a university lecturer was effectively over.

Mindfulness and meditation offers an alternative, and it's an attractive one. The relaxation meditation brings help with the emotional and physical symptoms of stress. The creativity which mindfulness and meditation brings also helps you get your work done more efficiently. Mindfulness and meditation helps to give you the perspective you need to stop the tunnel vision from having a total hold, and in doing so, gives you the psychological space to do things fundamentally differently. What a tonic!

Anxiety, Mindfulness and Meditation.

Anxiety is just another word for fear. If you are scared of something, if you are afraid, then the range of physical, emotional and thinking problems you experience is called anxiety. Anxiety is maintained by avoiding the thing you are scared of.

Sometimes the thing we are afraid of is clear, distinct and is a feature of the environment. This is called a phobia, and can be for just about anything, but tends to be restricted to spiders, snakes, dogs, needles, other people, open spaces and even imminent death.

What is often not understood is that we can also become scared of the contents of our own minds as well. Some people are scared of certain thoughts they might have. I had one client, for example, who was scared of imagining having sex with his mother. Another that milk bottles left on the street were contaminated by an imaginary stranger. People can also be scared of uncertainty, imperfection, failure - and even success.

Understanding that anxiety is a fear of something in the world or in your mind, it makes it possible to understand why avoiding the feared object will lead to maintaining the fear. By confronting the fear you may eventually learn that there is nothing to be scared of after all. If you avoid the fear, however, you will never learn this; all you will learn is that avoiding the feared object makes the fear go away, albeit temporarily.

Avoidance is possible when the feared object is in the world, like dogs, or buses, but what if we are scared of the contents of our mind? Well in these cases we can employ a whole range of techniques to avoid facing our fears. Worry is a good example. We are afraid of uncertainty and our ability to cope if things go wrong. In order to avoid the uncertainty, we fill the future with a range of scary 'what if' possibilities, and try to work out the solutions to these. Worry is a way of coping with one fear, by imagining another!

Cognitive behavioral therapists have become really good at helping people with their anxieties. However, they all come down to one thing; stopping avoiding the fear, and confronting it.

The biggest fear of my life, strangely enough, was other people. There have been times in my life when my social anxiety has got in the way of living a full life, like when I left home at 18 to go to work, and when I moved home again, at 21, to go to university to study psychology.

My childhood was less than perfect in many ways. My father was a particularly domineering man and was not short of telling me that I was a 'bloody idiot' with great regularity. I felt like I was always doing things wrong. Being a child I took my father's style of relating into the world, and treated everybody else as if they were 'bloody idiots' too. Not surprisingly, I didn't get much social success as a teen and young adult until I had worked this out. Like all social anxiety sufferers, it wasn't so much other people I was scared of; it was what they would think of me. In my case it was looking like a 'bloody idiot'!

I was still left with a high level of social unease, even after I left university and life became more settled. Eventually I decided to do something about it. If I was scared of looking like a 'bloody idiot', then I had to face the fear in the only way I could think of – I became a stand up comedian. Now my comedy skills will never be like a Billy Connelly or a Joan Rivers, that was never the point. Besides, I was never that interested in the comedy *per se*. The point was to look like a 'bloody idiot' and I'm pleased to say, as a standup comedian, I repeatedly succeeded!

Did it work? I can't say social situations with new people are my favorite places to be, but I faced my fear, and now understand it much better. I am now more self-confident as a result. Furthermore, I now know that even if I am 'a bloody idiot' in other people's eyes, I can survive ... it's actually not so bad.

Mindfulness and meditation offers an alternative to anxiety and fear, and it's an attractive one. First, meditation brings with it a sense of profound calm. One shouldn't meditate in order to achieve calm, or indeed judge the success of a meditation in terms of how relaxed you feel at the end. However, it is a fact that people who meditate, without even trying, build the capacity to experience calm. This is particularly important if you are scared by a number of things in your life, and find yourself in a more or less permanent anxiety state. As I often explain to my clients, meditation is a way of practicing what you want to become – calm – without having to worry too much about the problem – the thing you are scared of.

Meditation also brings about the mental space to observe your own emotional and mental processes. Without doubt if you are scared by something it will pop up into your meditation practice from time to time. You can then experience the anxiety process with full awareness. Eventually, like I did with social anxiety, you will know what you need to do to ease your suffering. You'll be pleased to know in most cases you won't have to do standup comedy!

Depression, Mindfulness and Meditation.

Of the three topics under discussion in this book, depression is the one I excelled at. I had bouts of depression as a child, as an adolescent, and as a young adult, several times. But after I fell ill with a swollen testicle, lost my job, my home and had to declare bankruptcy due to my ill health, I experienced a level of depression I had never experienced before. Literally years of my life passed barely able to do anything other than occasionally see friends and lie on the couch staring at the ceiling. There was little of 'Phil' left. I **was** the depression.

It was from this period of profound and all-consuming depression that meditation and mindfulness was able to help me recover. This is why I can say, with complete confidence, that, however bad things are for you right now, meditation and mindfulness can help.

Unfortunately my experience of repeated episodes of depression throughout my life is not uncommon. It seems that once a 'depressed mindset' has been established, it becomes easier and easier to slip back into it. Researchers have found that the single most important thing that 'rekindles' depression, and sets it off again, is rumination, that is to say, mindless dwelling on our problems, the failures of the past or worries about the future.

Depression itself is a range of symptoms that seemed to bundle together. All depressions are a mixture of some or all of these symptoms, but no two depression episodes, even in the same person, are ever the same. Here are some of the symptoms people who are depressed sometimes experience.

- Feeling sad, or low, all or most of the time.
- Feeling weepy for no reason.
- Low energy.
- Excessive sleepiness, and/or inability to sleep.
- Loss of motivation.
- Feeling helpless or powerless.
- Cynical about people and the world.
- Changes in appetite.
- Loss of interest in sex.
- Inability to start new tasks.
- Suicidal thoughts.

What could account for such a wide spread of apparently unconnected symptoms? There have been many theories put forward over the years. From my point of view, having seen depression from the inside and the outside, I believe an evolutionary perspective works best. In a tribal society, where 'depression' first evolved, if you were ill or frail, there would be a point where the energy that your kin needed to support you became simply too high to bear. At some point a calculus has to be made as to whether it is worth the group's effort keeping you, as a frail individual, alive.

I believe that depression is the mechanism that evolved to make this calculation. At some point we become too much of a burden, and slowly and steadily, we withdraw from social life and eventually, if left untreated, from life itself.

This behavior is much easier to see in animals. I had a pet dog as a child which became weaker and weaker. Eventually he walked off on his own, found a quiet place, and died.

This theory also accounts for one of the best treatments for depression: Behavioral reactivation. In this CBT therapy, the therapist encourages the client to start re-engaging with the world, and supports them to do so. As I understand it, this is the exact opposite of the depression process itself. It boils down to doing fun things with people you like.

Mindfulness and meditation, however, offers an alternative, and it's an attractive one. By practicing being in the moment, we are doing the one thing we need to do to stop ourselves getting into a depression, or deepening it if we are already in one. Being in the moment is the opposite of rumination. In rumination, it is as if we are caught up in our own thoughts, and they seem to have a life of their own. Mindfulness gets you out of that ruminating mental space, and into the real world - out of your head, and into your body.

Helping to control rumination was the central idea behind Mindfulness Based Cognitive Therapy for depression (Segal, Williams and Teasdale, 2002). They reasoned that if you can control rumination, you could prevent depression relapse.

But can mindfulness and meditation help if you are depressed right now? We will talk more about depressed mind states in coming chapters, but the simple answer is yes. The more aware you become that 'you are doing depression right now', then you have a greater degree of choice as to continue 'doing' the depression, or do something fun instead. You might choose to feel the comfort of despair, but choosing depression already feels different to being depressed without choice, or awareness.

The Relationship Between Stress, Anxiety and Depression.

There is a tradition in mental health care of trying to separate mental health problems into discrete 'disease' categories. There would be one category for stress, one for anxiety, and one for depression (in fact the latest diagnostic criteria allow for multiple sub-divisions within each of these broad categories).

My own experience, and the experience of working with my clients, is that these may be helpful for professionals to communicate with each other, but rarely help clients. In reality, it is difficult not to be anxious if you have too much to do and/or feel in danger of 'failing'. Similarly, if you are anxious and scared by the world, it's difficult not to be stressed out. Similarly if you are stressed and/or anxious for any length of time, it is difficult not to feel fed up. If you are fed up for long enough ... you're depressed.

Stress, anxiety and depression, in short, tend to come as a package. I will continue to refer to these categories to help get my points across, but I want to end this chapter by making the point that if you are stressed, anxious or depressed, you have one thing in common. You're in 'reactive mind'. And it is to this I will turn in the next chapter.

Before I talk about reactive mind, I just want to check in with where I am up to on this writing / meditation retreat. I'm really pleased with my progress. Everything you have read so far has been written in the last two days. I'm starting to get into the flow of things a little. I've only done three of the planed six meditations and I haven't been jogging yet. But that's OK. I have done a mindful shave, mindful shower, and earlier I did a mindful walk on the beach, which was amazing. I'm excited to tell you about my experiences, but that's for later. I also feel I am starting to 'wake up' a little bit. The world is starting to appear a little more interconnected, and my senses are recovering their acuity. I'm starting to notice things like art on the wall I had just walked past only yesterday. The people I interact with are now warmer toward me, no doubt because I am being more kind to them. It feels good to be me right now.

Then, only moments later, disaster! I broke my rule and used my mobile phone. I couldn't make contact with a close friend, and became increasingly irritated. She was 'obviously' ignoring me. It was if I had defaulted to my pre-vacation stressed mind. I started to think the last two days had been a waste of time. I don't want to be in this stressed frame of mind, and I now blamed her for it. I gave up writing and tried to get some sleep.

The next day. Because I was so irritated last night, I couldn't sleep, which meant I overslept, and again it was my friend's fault. At night I began wondering (ruminating!) why I was in a friendship with someone who obviously doesn't care for me. I started ruminating about punishing her with no more texts for the next two weeks. I feel tired, agitated and angry.

Then after a meditation, it occurred to me that actually this is really cool. This situation provides exactly the right information I need to illustrate the next chapter! Suddenly I find myself asking if it is me that is writing this book, or the universe?

3.
Reactive Mind, and its Alternative.

I'm writing this on day three and despite a good start I seem to have stalled. The issue over contacting my friend got resolved. It was a technical fault receiving texts with international roaming. In other words, there was nothing personal about it. Yet my head made it so. I had become really upset.

There is a moral to this story. One, is that when you go 'on retreat', with no one to talk to, even really small issues seem to take on a life of their own. I remember going on a week long summer retreat at Dhanakosa, a beautiful retreat center located in stunning rugged Scottish mountains. One afternoon someone had moved something close to where I meditated in the meditation room. My mind became obsessed. Why had they moved it? What were they trying to say to me by moving it? Needless to say the whole retreat was in complete silence, so I couldn't talk about it with anyone. I knew I was being paranoid, but I couldn't get the narrative out of my head. It took two days before I got back to normal. I learnt a lot about how my head does paranoia on that retreat!

I feel a similar thing has happened here. In one sense it was nothing: my friend was sending texts and I wasn't receiving them, but the whole thing spiraled out of my control. Meditation isn't necessarily easy. Your mental processes become transparent to you. You can go very deep, and sometimes need a lot of courage to stick with it. It would have been easy to entertain myself in the bar, or turn on a television. It's not that there is anything wrong with these things. But they would have been a distraction. In choosing to come to Tunisia, I had chosen something different. I had chosen to write and meditate.

Yes, I've had a good start, but I've had a wobble and got off track a little bit. With the issue of the texts resolved, I feel I need to gather my energies and have a bit more compassion for myself. I'm going to do two half-hour meditations to help me with this. The first, the mindfulness of breathing, I'll do to gather my energies. I write about this in Chapter 6. Needless to say if your mind is scattered and unfocussed, the mindfulness of breathing is great to help center you and calm the body and mind. The second, the metta bhavana, the loving kindness meditation, I'll use to develop some compassion for me and my friend. I write about this in Chapter 7.

In this chapter we are going to get deep into some of the reactive thinking habits of the mind. This is the everyday routine thinking that most of us don't even pay attention to, yet it profoundly affects how we view the world, and how we feel about the world. If you seriously want to help yourself with your stress, anxiety and depression, this chapter is the one you need to master.

In this chapter I will describe in some detail twelve thinking habits my clients often present with. I want to state at the outset that there is nothing intrinsically wrong with thinking in these ways. On the contrary, they are simply the way the mind works. To think is, in many respects unless we are particularly careful, to fall into these reactive thinking habits. It cannot be otherwise.

At this point I imagine that most of you have an intuitive idea of what thinking habits might be, and are maybe even aware of some of your own unhelpful ones, but what do I mean by 'reactive'?

In some ways it's better to start with what reactive thinking is not. Have you ever been on a beach with nothing to do but spend the day soaking up the sun and being completely absorbed by just being? If beach life isn't your thing, have you ever been on a long journey and drifted into a peaceful state where time itself seems to disappear? Well this is what I am going to call 'creative mind'. When you are in creative mind you are first and foremost deeply relaxed. In terms of your nervous system, you are dominated by the ventral vagal system. When you are in this state your powers of thought are at their height. You can move flexibly and creatively through whatever you turn your attention to. Problem solving is easy, as creative solutions just seem to appear.

Lets just reflect about where I was yesterday when I was feeling good. When I talked of going to the beach, and all being well with my world, I was in what I'm calling creative mind ... and I felt great! In fact when most people talk about feeling good, they are in this relaxed creative place.

So this is creative mind. But what of 'reactive mind'. Well this is in some ways the complete opposite. When I got into a row with my friend in my head, I had shifted to full on 'reactive mind'. My thoughts seemed to control me, and, I must emphasize, the reality it created seemed compelling and miserable. I felt stressed, was worried about my future relationship with her, and was deeply frustrated. In fact because it was so compelling, it had me well and truly hooked in.

This is the reactive part, like one domino falling in a row after another, one thought seemed to cause the next to arise and I was off. Like being on the Circle Line in London, a tube track that is literally a circle circumnavigating central London, I was going round and round and round, unable to get off. If you recall, it stopped me from getting off to sleep, and this had a knock on effect for today.

As you may well imagine, I'm not in reactive mind anymore, and the teachings of this book will help you to unhook yourself from that particular caravan of hell. But first things first.

What is reactive mind? Well it is what happens to the mind when it perceives a threat. In days of old this may have been the proverbial sabre-toothed tiger, but in our modern world, like it was for me yesterday, it is more likely to be something I thought up myself. Something imagined.

At school many of us were taught about the fight or flight reaction. We were taught that animals, when faced with danger, organize their bodily resources to fight or run from the threat. Blood moves from our gut to the muscles, our heart rate quickens, adrenalin starts pumping through our veins, we become more alert …. Sounds a lot like stress and anxiety, and of course it is. When we say we are stressed or anxious, what we are saying, in biological terms, is that we have switched to fight or flight mode.

What we were not taught at school was that the fight or flight mode also has profound psychological consequences. We literally think differently when we are stressed, anxious or depressed. Our thinking becomes more 'chunky' and 'automatic'; it has to after all, we are, in danger.

People who work in the emergency business know this well. For example fire doors that always open outward from the building to safety. The reason for this is that if fire doors opened inward, people would die while pushing the door outward, never thinking that the door opened inward. In the fight or flight mode, we lose the ability to be creative. We need to make snap decisions, even if a proportion of those decisions go disastrously wrong for some of the people, some of the time.

What I want to suggest is that when we are stressed, anxious or depressed, we cannot help but perceive the world as threatening. As a consequence we drop out of creative thinking and into reactive thinking. Since there are not many sabre-toothed tigers about these days, we probably are reacting to a threat in our own imagination. However, as I pointed out earlier, reactive thinking is designed to get us out of danger, its 'chunkier' and less nuanced. It's not the kind of thinking we need onboard to solve our subtle, and often imaginary, threats of modern social living.

If we were being kind to ourselves, we would get out of the threat activation system and into the ventral vagal system as quickly as we possibly could so we can re-evaluate the scenario with our flexible, creative mind. As you saw with me yesterday, once the reactive mind is activated, it feels real; the version of the world it creates is deeply compelling. The fact I love my friend deeply meant nothing yesterday as I defended myself against the perceived slight of (maybe) not returning a text.

So let's get under the bonnet of our minds and look at some of these chunky, fight or flight, or as I call it, 'reactive' mental habits. Beware though; this list is by no means exhaustive. These are the ones that seem to me to be most common.

1. **Catastrophizing.**

    Was I catastrophizing yesterday? Just a bit. I had gone from not receiving a text to "I'm not loved" in an instant. I had jumped right back into reactive mind.

    What is important to stress when talking about catastrophizing and other reactive habits of mind, is that when you are in the grip of them, they feel compelling. It's not as if you have the thoughts, are able to hold them lightly, knowing you are making a thinking habit. Well maybe sometimes you can, but invariably the thinking habit produces the reality as perceived. Yesterday I wasn't receiving texts, and that was because I wasn't loved. That **was** my reality. If thinking habits were not so compelling and persistent, they would be easy to dismiss. But they are not.

    Just about every client I have ever worked with catastrophizes some or all of their experience. It's part of being human. But each of us learns to catastrophize in different situations. One client I worked with catastrophized whenever he saw an email from his brother in his inbox. Another catastrophized whenever he felt the twinge of pain anywhere in his body. It is as if at a very deep level we get a stimulus response pair set up, a mind program that is then difficult to break. If X then catastrophize! Phobias are essentially catastrophic thinking patterns. IF spider THEN die!

Indeed, there are often good reasons for why such IF THEN rules form. In the case of my clients, occasionally emails from my first client's brother did bring bad news, and in the latter case, a twinge of pain would invariably set of weeks of worrying about his health. In my case, I'm super sensitive to evidence of rejection from friends due to an insecure attachment style. If I started talking about that though, we would end up with another book! My rule, however, is IF small rejection THEN feel massively unloved.

What is important with catastrophizing, and other thinking styles, is that eventually we calm down from our original reactive mind state, and we can start to see that our behavior fitted a catastrophizing habit pattern. This process is itself an act of mindfulness. It is paying attention to our experiences. Once we start doing so, and can identify habit patterns within our experience, the power the thinking habit has over us starts to lose its compelling nature. Once that happens, the space arrives to view the world in a more balanced way. We develop, in other words, the space to be other than stressed, depressed or anxious. We could do something else instead. Maybe we could be compassionate with ourselves for over reacting for understandable reasons?

If you practice the mindfulness techniques in this book, you will become increasingly able to spot your catastrophizing. When you do, ask yourself if you are really in life threatening danger.

If you are not, maybe a more nuanced approach would be more effective.

2. **Denial of 'what is'.**

When we talk about 'denial' in everyday language, we often refer to the big things. If someone has a terminal diagnosis from the doctor, and understandably is finding the information difficult to deal with, we say they are 'in denial'.

The way I am using the term, however, is for the little things as well. It is for the here and now experience of ourselves being in a feeling state we don't want to be in. Last night I was denying my feeling state. I had been in such a good place, I was happy, and I had a glow of pride that I had got so much written so quickly, then pop. My mood shifted. I was stressed, and I didn't want to be there. I wanted to be in the happy state. I was in denial of where my feeling tone had taken me.

In principle, the feeling tone of our experience can either be positive, negative or neutral. Sometimes, even invariably, this can be very subtle indeed. Later in the book I will suggest some exercises for becoming more mindful of subtle feeling states. Why is this important? Well instinctively, or perhaps I should say, reactively, we move towards positive feeling states and want more, and we move away, with aversion, from negative feeling states. Both can be problematic.

How can an instinctive move towards a positive feeling state be a bad thing? Well the point here is it is often done without awareness, and the consequences can be damaging for us in the long term. Take sugar as an example. For most of us, sugar gives us a very subtle but positive feeling tone. That's why processed food invariably contains sugar, or even worse, artificial sweetener. If we are not very careful, we end up eating processed foods all the time, simply unaware we are getting the sugar hit. In fact the whole of modern marketing works by creating subtle positive feeling tones for every conceivable product. Children are most susceptible to this, of course, which is why marketers often work through the children to get to the parents.

Aversion from negative feeling tones can also cause us problems if we are not fully aware of what is happening. One easy place to see this happening is in relationship with other people. In relationship to some people, for whatever reason, we get a negative feeling tone. We might not even register it as a thought; we just know that we feel better around Billy rather than Kelly. We then usually, and unreflectively, attribute that to a stable feature of them. You then feel justified in liking Billy but not Kelly. But hold on! The feeling tone, and the attraction and aversion that came with it, was something happening inside me. In principle, it might have nothing to do with either Billy or Kelly. If we are not careful, our reactive, unthinking mind ends up choosing our friends for us. Now that's scary.

If you practice the mindfulness techniques in this book, you will become increasingly able to spot your denial of what is. When you do, ask yourself if you are really in life threatening danger. If you are not, maybe a more nuanced approach would be more effective.

3. **Misplaced responsibility.**

Generally in life, if something goes right or wrong, it is either due to things I have done, or things someone else has done, or perhaps even nobody's responsibility. What is remarkable is that, as individuals, we develop habits for the attribution of responsibility, irrespective of whose responsibility it actually was. So for example I'm aware that if ever I've lost something, it's always because someone else has moved it. It could never be because I misplaced the item! Today I couldn't find my moisturizer, and immediately and reactively, blamed the maid. Another common one is people are often quick to take responsibility if things have gone well, and blame others if things go wrong. Indeed whole cultures can be placed on this continuum.

Sometimes though, the consequences of this thought habit is not so funny. If your style is to blame yourself for everything, you are going to batter down your self-esteem. SImilarly if you never take responsibility for your actions, you will end up living in a Walter Mitty style existence.

I observe this with the clients I work with as a psychotherapist. Some clients know they have got themselves into a hole, and they are looking for support and guidance to help them get out of it. The key here is that this type of client knows that they are responsible for their problems, and that they are responsible for getting themselves out of them. My role is as a kind of cheerleader from the wings, supporting them and encouraging to do so.

Then there are clients who fall into the other extreme. They have problems because of the bad things other people have done, or are doing to them. What they are looking for in me is someone who will sort all this out for them, and make them feel better. The key here is that this type of client is not responsible for their problems, and someone else is responsible for 'fixing' them. My role is as some kind of technical expert, who rewires their mind for them, and makes everything go away.

As you can imagine, the first kind of client is easy to work with, and makes rapid progress. The second kind of client is a nightmare to work with, takes years before we get anywhere, and often drops out before therapy reaches its goals.

So I've created two straw people here. But here's the deal; in different areas of our lives we all can be habitually and reactively *both* people. For example we may take responsibility at work, but not at home.

Again, it cannot be stressed too much how compelling these realities feel. It is as if it really is 'my fault' or 'their fault' in any given situation. It is only by bringing compassionate, mindfulness and creative awareness to the situation that we can see we are making huge mistakes.

If you practice the mindfulness techniques in this book, you will become increasingly able to spot your misplaced responsibility and its impact. When you do, ask yourself if you are really in life threatening danger. If you're not, maybe a more nuanced approach would be more effective.

4. **Black and white thinking.**

When I introduced the idea of reactive thinking styles, I did so within the context of them being a kind of cognitive shortcut, chunky, but suitable for use in emergency situations. Black and white, or all or nothing thinking, is the chunky emergency thinking style *par excellence*.

Imagine you are in tropical climes, you are relaxing in your hammock, and in the corner of your eye you see something slither towards you. Immediately you think 'snake', jump out of the hammock and run.

This is a classic example of how the fight and flight, threat activation system works to keep you safe. What it relied on was the thinking habit of black and white or all or nothing thinking. You reacted as if it were a snake. If you would have responded with your creative mind, and allowed the possibility of 'snake', and the possibility of 'no snake' to comingle, it would be all over for you; the snake would have bitten, and you'd be dead soon after. Black and white thinking is crude, after all it might just have been a twig moved by the wind, but it keeps us safe in an emergency.

As we talked about in a previous chapter, the world we live in is not designed with our emotional wellbeing at heart. We no longer have the comfort of living in socially well-established and stable extended kin networks. The world we live in is inherently more unpredictable than our evolutionary cousins experienced. It is unsurprising that the fight and flight, threat activation system is triggering all the time. What this means is our cognition, the picture we form of the world, is being pushed into black and white categories more often than ever before. It is unsurprising, for example, in times of economic upheaval, politically we become more extreme. Instinctively we feel safer in such times with politicians who use simple categories. It doesn't mean to say we are in fact safer in the hands, of say, nationalist politicians, but we feel safer.

And this is the rub; in the world our thinking habits create for us, we move towards what feels safer, rather than what is actually safer. In reality, modern industrialized nations have the lowest violent death rates in history. You may have felt safer in the middle ages, but you were actually in more danger.

If you practice the mindfulness techniques in this book, you will become increasingly able to spot your black and white, all or nothing thinking in real time. When you do, ask yourself if you are really in life threatening danger. If you're not, maybe a more nuanced approach would be more effective.

5. Over generalizing.

In the example of the texts yesterday when my mood collapsed, perhaps my biggest reactive thinking problem was moving from a particular situation, 'my friend hasn't returned my texts', to a general situation, 'I will never be happy with my friends, they all treat me badly'. This is an example of overgeneralizing, and, as human beings, we do it all the time.

Over generalizing is tied to the philosophical problem of induction. An example of the problem of induction might be the sun rising tomorrow. Even though I know the sun has risen every morning for recorded history, how can I be sure it will rise again tomorrow?

You will be pleased to know I won't offer you a philosophical response. Rather my concern is more practical. As a matter of routine practical cognition, if we see something happening once, we assume it is part of a generalizable pattern, and the same thing will continue to happen in the future.

Now if we are stressed, anxious or depressed, and our thinking has become 'chunky', we have something of a problem. We are more likely to see the specific example we find threatening, as the pattern that will keep repeating. If it is going to keep repeating, then, as in my case, I have to end the friendship, right?

In a real emergency, of course, we want our minds to work like this. If a fire is burning in the building, it makes sense to assume it will continue to where I'm sleeping. If a bear is running towards me, it makes sense to assume it will keep running towards me until it gets to me!

If you practice the mindfulness techniques in this book, you will become increasingly able to spot your over generalizing in real time. When you do, ask yourself if you are really in life threatening danger. If you're not, maybe a more nuanced approach would be more effective.

6. Emotional reasoning.

As I'm often fond of saying to my clients, this is my favorite habit of mind. The reason is simply because I fall foul of it so often myself. Essentially it's a simple idea. We reason from how we feel to reality. So for example, if I feel stressed, I assume that all this stuff really must get done. If I feel scared, I assume there really is something to be scared of. If I feel depressed, then I assume I/the future/the world is really bad.

Emotional reasoning also comes into more subtle feelings. Remember I suggested that all moments are imbued with either a subtle positive, neutral or negative emotional tone. We might not even be consciously aware of these emotional tones, but we nonetheless judge the world, often inaccurately, by these tones. One way of looking at 'waking up', or even 'enlightenment' itself, is being aware of these subtle emotional tones, and not drawing false inferences from them.

When we are stressed, anxious or depressed, we have to be really careful of generalizing from our feeling state to reality. If we are stressed, we may conclude that the work really does need to be done. If we are anxious, we might conclude that the thing we are scared of really is scary. If we are depressed, we may conclude that because we feel awful about ourselves, the future and the world, that we, the future, or the world really is bad.

If you practice the mindfulness techniques in this book, you will become increasingly able to spot your emotional reasoning. When you do, ask yourself if you are really in life threatening danger. If you are not, maybe a more nuanced approach would be more effective.

7. **Broken Rules.**

When we were little children, we were taught rules to keep us safe. "Don't touch the cooker, it's hot"; "Don't run into the street, it's dangerous". As we get older, our parents teach us more subtle rules about who we are, and our place in the world. I learnt "when you are 18 you go to university"; "we vote Labour in our family". Indeed, as we get older, we start adding our own rules to the list. These rules give us a sense of predictability and stability about how the world behaves - even a sense of who we are, our identities.

Each of these rules, however, comes with a habit energy attached. When we are stressed, anxious and depressed, and unable to react creatively, these rules become more rigid, like absolute truths. They become our shoulds, oughts, musts, have tos etc.

What happens if one of our rules gets broken, say by us, or other people? Well we get angry. Anger is the emotion we feel when our expectations of ourselves and other people, our rules, are not met.

So it's sort of a double whammy. Being stressed, anxious or depressed, we rest more absolutely on our rules of living, and as a consequence lose our flexibility and creativity. We then get angrier with ourselves and other people when our rules are broken, making us more stressed, anxious or depressed.

If you practice the mindfulness techniques in this book, you will become increasingly able to spot your broken rules in real time. When you do, ask yourself if you are really in life threatening danger. If you are not, maybe a more nuanced approach would be more effective.

8. **Automatic Attention Selection Bias.**

If we expect something bad is going to happen, we look out for it. This is just common sense. But if we look out for something, aren't we also more likely to find it? Of course we are.

Have you ever had the experience of buying something you thought was really cool, then on the way home seeing other people with the same item. I had this experience with my current car. By the end of the first week I was sick of seeing red Peugeot 207 cc's.

What I'm discussing here is called an automatic attention selection bias, and it works habitually for more subtle things, as well as the more obvious. What is important to note about these selection biases, is that once set, they generate examples automatically. This is what they are designed to do. This is what happened with my car. I wasn't looking for other red Peugeot 207 cc's, they just kept popping into my awareness without me even trying.

These automatic attention selection biases are really important in understanding stress, anxiety and depression, so bear with me as I go through this.

Let's take anxiety first. If you suffer from health anxiety you tend to worry a lot about your health. What kind of automatic attention selection bias is likely to be set up for you by your mind? Well you're going to notice, automatically without you even thinking, things that look like symptoms of illnesses. Things like lumps, bumps, pains and aches.

Let's take another anxiety people often have, social anxiety. Here people worry that they are going to look foolish, or something similar, in social situations. What kind of automatic attention selection bias is going to be set up for such a person? Well you're going to notice all your little social *faux pas*. Things like slips of the tongue, stuttering, blushing, awkward silences, etc.

So if that's how it works for anxiety, what about stress? Well stress tends to be experienced by people who have too much to do, and feel they can't cope with it. What kind of automatic attention selection bias is going to be set up for such a person? Well they are going to pay attention to all the things they haven't done (rather than the things they have done), and they are going to pay attention to all their little mistakes (rather than all the times they get things right).

I imagine you are getting the idea by now. Automatic attention selection biases end up confirming exactly what people are concerned about in the first place! All the evidence that disconfirms their concern is simply ignored. How mad is that!

Of course it is exactly the same with depression. In order to be depressed you pretty much have to have either a negative view of yourself, your future or the world. If that's what you believe, the magic of the automatic attention selection bias goes to work, and starts generating all the evidence you would ever need to confirm that view of yourself, your future or the world. Of course you then completely ignore any evidence to the contrary.

If you practice the mindfulness techniques in this book, you will become increasingly able to spot your automatic attention selection biases. When you do, ask yourself if you are really in life threatening danger. If you're not, maybe a more nuanced approach would be more effective.

I'm now half way through what is turning out to be a long chapter. I feel like I've been through a lot so far this week. I did the double meditation I mentioned earlier. It went really well. Even though I meditated for over an hour, with a short break half way through, the time passed really quickly.

Just so you know, I had one gin and tonic last night, and I haven't been jogging yet. Maybe tomorrow. I have avoided talking to people though. I exchange greetings with the waiter and the bar man who serves me my water, and, I'm sorry to say, my coffee (which is turning into my treat of this writing retreat).

I am, however, feeling a little bored right now. It feels like I've got a long way to go. This whole process is heavy for me at the moment. In terms of my overall feeling tone, it is negative. I need to boost my mood and my motivation, so I will do the metta bhavana and attempt to connect emotionally a little more deeply with you. You will learn all about the metta bhavana meditation in Chapter 7. All you need to know now is that on this occasion I've chosen to work with five people (other than myself) to coincide with what I imagine to be five different types of reader.

1. The person who is interested in the meditation, and less so the psychology.
2. The person who is interested in the psychology, and less so the meditation.
3. The person who is profoundly stressed.
4. The person who is profoundly anxious.
5. The person who is profoundly depressed.

Well I did it, and it was quite profound. I feel the universe came under my flagging wings, and lifted me up a little bit. My visual perception has also shifted. Everything seems clearer, sharper, and colors are fuller and deeper. I also feel I touched deeply a concern that would be held by all of the five possible readers. So now I will be able to write and rewrite more clearly with each reader in mind.

I also became more creative. I realized that if I'm flagging writing this chapter, simply write another chapter instead. I can always come back to this one another day. I also realized if I needed a break, or even a gin and tonic, then it's OK to have one. This book will not be motivating if I write it with a demotivated voice. I suppose I not only connected more deeply with my readers' needs, I also became more in touch with my own needs.

Now, back to the chapter ...

9. **Discount the positives.**

Have you ever received a compliment, and refused to accept it? Well what's going on here is a form of discounting the positives. This is not the same as having a negative automatic selection bias; this is a deliberate action – a refusal to accept what is. It is a positive choice to reject the positives in your life! It is more common than you may think.

I come from England, and the North of England at that. Europe, England, and the North of England in particular, have an in built cultural bias of rejecting the positives, at least compared to North American populations.

If you go skiing in North America, in a ski lift queue, some talented young thing backflips over a jump, you're likely to get spontaneous rounds of applause, and shouts of "Cool man". If the same happened in Europe, people would feign not to notice, and even mutter 'poser' under their breath.

Europeans do not celebrate success. In England we see celebrating success as a vice. In the North of England it's worse. We celebrate our failures!

Surely this is madness! And you would be right. If western psychology has learnt anything in the last one hundred years, it is positive reinforcement, i.e. praise, which shapes behavior. Why would you focus on your failures, when focusing on your successes is so much better for you? Well many of us do, and we blame our culture for it!

Can we get more of a balance here? It is one thing bragging about our successes to covet social prestige. It is another, quietly acknowledging our own and our friends' and families' successes. The former is a kind of narcissism, the latter, I would suggest, is good mental hygiene. My message is clear hear: don't discount the positives in your life, learn to celebrate them, albeit appropriately. If your friends and family won't celebrate your positives with you ... get people in your life that will.

If you practice the mindfulness techniques in this book, you will become increasingly able to spot when you discount the positives. When you do, ask yourself if you are really in life threatening danger. If you are not, maybe a more nuanced approach would be more effective.

10. **Full of Ego.**

When we are in a relaxed, creative frame of mind, the world reveals itself as it is. When I went for a mindful beach walk the other day, I was able to see two spiders scurry across the sand. I was transfixed. Although 10 cm or so apart, one appeared to be following the other. It was as if they were joined in some way, as if they were a couple. "I" was not there, there was simply the sand and the spiders and a curiosity in the behavior they exhibited. My ego, or sense of self, had disappeared. I was in creative mind.

The minute my mood shifted because my friend appeared not

to respond to my texts, I was back in reactive mind. The "I" became load and center stage. "I" had been affronted. "I" was being ignored. "I" was being disrespected.

Our reactive mind needs this sense of "I". Our ego is never so present as when we are stressed. It is the "I", after all, that is in danger. But when we are relaxed, things soften. It is as if we hold ourselves a little less tightly, and allow ourselves, and the world, to reveal itself more subtly. We can simply "be". And this is enough.

If you practice the mindfulness techniques in this book, you will become increasingly able to spot your moves into ego. When you do, ask yourself if you are really in life threatening danger. If you are not, maybe a more nuanced approach would be more effective.

11. Rumination.

Rumination, endlessly thinking about the past, the future or the present, is intimately caught up with stress, anxiety and depression.

If you are stressed, no doubt you obsess about all the things you haven't done, and the consequences of not doing them. If you are depressed, you can equally dwell for hours ruminating on past pains or dwelling on the 'hopeless' future. The same is true of people who are anxious. In fact worry is the endless running through of possible negative scenarios and how you could deal with them.

The operative word here is endless, without end. The more time you throw at ruminating, the more it will take. What is worse, the more you ruminate, the more time you spend in the threat activation system, the more you will immerse yourself in your problems, rather than getting into creative mind, and actually solving them.

So why do people ruminate? Well there are two answers to this. The first is that people mistake rumination for problem solving. Problem solving starts with a definition of the problem. It then proceeds to the creative consideration of a range of possible solutions. A solution is decided upon, and the first action toward the solution is taken. The problem is then forgotten. It is journey, with a beginning, middle and end.

Rumination goes round and round. Often, if you were to start problem solving by simply defining the problem, it would be all over. Often there is simply no problem. So this leads to the next reason why people ruminate. Even though it causes them pain to do so, it gives them a perverse satisfaction. Buried in all that pain is a nugget of pleasure. The pleasure comes in being the pain - A proof of one's own existence. Without the pain, very often, people are scared that they might not even exist. This is revealed in statements like, "You need to understand what an awful childhood I had in order to understand **who I am**". If you believe this, you are stuffed. You have to endlessly keep revisiting old pain, keeping yourself distressed, because that's how you create **who you are**.

Rumination, of course, recruits a very useful capacity of the mind: the ability to abstract from the now to learn from the past and plan the future. Such a skill is really helpful if used wisely, as in a genuine emergency. The rest of the time, it is a distraction from actually living fully and creatively right now. Think about it. Has worrying about the future ever brought you happiness in the present? Has reflecting on previous failures ever made you happy in the now? Of course it hasn't. It is just a reactive habit of mind we use to keep us distressed. But there is an alternative.

If you practice the mindfulness techniques in this book, you will become increasingly able to spot your rumination in real time. When you do, ask yourself if you are really in life threatening danger. If you are not, maybe a more nuanced approach would be more effective.

12. The Intrinsic Meaning Fallacy.

When I was a psychology undergraduate, I was taught a study concerning astrology which stuck with me. People were asked their date of birth, and on that basis horoscopes were prepared for them. Remarkably a large proportion of the horoscopes were judged to be an accurate description by the person. What is more remarkable was that all the people received the same horoscope!

What is going on here? Well it is something I call the 'intrinsic meaning' fallacy. That is to say, we examine the world as if the events in the world are of intrinsic meaning. We saw it on the first day when I was at breakfast and when I looked up the woman looked away. I interpreted her 'turning away' as intrinsically meaningful, 'obviously' she was disapproving of my tattoos!

The truth is that in an emergency situation, it is wise to treat everything as intrinsically meaningful. If we don't pay attention we might miss something. But when we are in creative mind this softens. It is as if we are quite content to just let 'stuff' happen. Which is how it should be.

An example of this was when I arrived in the hotel earlier in the week. I was a little concerned about what other people might think of me travelling alone. I interpreted the minutiae of what people did in relationship to that. In other words I treated everything the waiters, and the other guests, did, as intrinsically meaningful in relationship to me. The truth, of course, is that even if they correctly guessed I was travelling alone, any reaction they may have towards that would say more about them than me. However compelling it felt at the time, I was not, and never would be, the center of their world.

If you practice the mindfulness techniques in this book, you will become increasingly able to spot the intrinsic meaning fallacy in real time. When you do, ask yourself if you are really in life threatening danger. If you are not, maybe a more nuanced approach would be more effective.

It sounds like a lot to take in at once I know. For most of us, most of the time, we tend to be quite predictable and use the same habits again and again. You probably were reflecting on what habits of thought you use regularly as you were reading through the list. If not, take some time to reflect now on which ones apply to you, and which ones less so. Over the next few days, bear them in mind to see if you were right.

How Understanding Reactive Mind Habits Helps.

Here's the deal: if you are stressed, anxious or depressed you are in reactive mind probably all the time. Possibly you have been in reactive for years, and only have a vague idea things could be otherwise. If you want to stand the best chance of resolving your problems, you need to be in creative mind. But that's not easy.

I remember when I was revising for my final exams for my psychology degree. I had worked really hard to position myself for a 1st class honors degree. By the end of working really hard for three years, I was exhausted. I was struggling to find the energy to study. My mind saw the 'threat' of the valued goal, the 1st, slipping away from me. I lived in a stressed out, anxiety driven and demoralized world for what seemed like an eternity.

I do remember one thing from that period. I went for a walk to my local, overgrown 17th century cemetery. It was, and still is, one of my favorite places. The sun baked down on me, on the tombstones, and on the foliage that was obscuring them. As I walked through the cemetery I read the names and occupations of those who had passed away, often tragically young by modern standards, and wondered what their lives had been like.

As if from nowhere it felt like a veil lifted, and with it my anxiety and stress. I felt a deep inner peace. I knew, from a larger perspective, what I was worried about didn't really matter. Then as quickly as it had arrived the veil descended again, and I was back to my stressed anxious and demoralized self.

At the time it baffled me. Now I know I simply moved from reactive mind into creative mind, and then back again. However I never forgot the capacity of the mind to suddenly and miraculously 'wake up' from suffering. This book, in some ways, is a footnote to that experience.

What now follows in the rest of this book is a regimen of truth to help you do what happened to me far too briefly, to wake up from suffering.

4.
Challenging Negative Reactive Habits of Thought.

You may well be thinking at this point, how does understanding my thinking patterns help? Well, if you can be mindful of your reactive thinking habits, you can, in time, come to spot them in real time. If you can come to do that, when you are distressing yourself with your reactive mind, you can just ask yourself, is there really anything to be so upset with about now? And if not, you will be able to just drop your reactive mind, as you would drop hot coals if they were burning you.

The first stage is to become aware of the thinking habits themselves. Now some people I work with find this quite easy. If I ask them to record all their negative thinking between sessions, the next time I see them, they appear with pages and pages of negativity, all beautifully captured in glorious Technicolor.

It is more usual, however, for people to struggle to some extent in becoming aware of their negative thinking habits. If you reflect on this a moment the reason is obvious. If you were aware of what you were doing, you would just stop, right? Nobody, after all, would choose unnecessary suffering for himself or herself.

What this means is that your negative thinking habits are running in the background. Just as the computer I'm typing into only has one program open at the moment, the word processor, I know that it is running other programs in the background, but I'm just not aware of them. There's the clock, for example: I'm connected to the internet, so the computer is monitoring that, and I have a virus checker, which is running in the background too.

It's the same with our mind. Ordinarily we actually want our mind to run automatically in the background. We simply would not get much achieved if we had to consciously think about everything, all at the same time. Imagine what it would be like if I had the word processor running at the same time as the clock, at the same time as the virus checker and the internet, etc. My screen would get pretty confusing, and I would feel overwhelmed.

It's the same with our minds. Routine tasks, like sorting out what is relevant to process, and how to process the relevant stuff, is largely done without our conscious involvement. Of course this is fine, if 'the reality', these automatic processes are creating is a useful one. But what if it keeps pulling out things to get stressed, anxious or down about? If your mind keeps telling you that you are in danger, you are going to stay in these chunky, inefficient processing modes, and keep using them to create your reality. You are never going to escape unless you do something drastic.

So the first thing is to start to become more aware of what is going on in the background. At first, like most of my clients, you might struggle. But that's OK. The more you practice the better you will get. By the time you get to week 10 of The Enlightenment Plan, you will be so good at spotting your unhelpful negative thinking patterns, you will just smile when they appear. Awareness literally robs them of their hold over you. It takes away their power.

So mindfulness and meditation is key, and that is what I will go on to discuss in the next chapter, but there is more you can do to help you with your negative thinking patterns. And that is finding a healthier alternative to using them.

There is a general rule I have when working with my clients, and that is if I'm going to invite a client to stop doing something unhelpful, they need to be able to substitute something helpful in its place.

Imagine you have an alcohol problem. Obviously you need to stop hanging round pubs and clubs, and going to those welcoming friends who always crack open a bottle of wine, etc. Now if you have an alcohol problem, you probably spent a lot of time hanging out round these places and people. If you suddenly cut them all out, life would be pretty bleak and uninteresting. You would be hanging around wishing you could have a drink. So you need alternatives: the gym, take up martial arts, fell walking, skiing, chess, poetry classes, painting. In fact anything will do, so long as you find it interesting, and it doesn't involve alcohol.

It's the same with your mind. At the moment it has these unhelpful thinking patterns that relentlessly generate stress, fear and sadness. If you want your mind to work differently, yes you have to get it to stop doing these things, and the best way of doing that is to give it something else to do that is more helpful.

Now you may be saying, 'but Phil, my life really is too full, too scary or too hopeless'. Well remember, it is the nature of your reactive mind to make the reality compelling and urgent. It is designed for emergencies, so it shouts 'top priority' at you and 'this is really true'. The reality your reactive mind creates is designed to be compelling. But here's the deal: it doesn't make it true. You are probably not in danger. Even if you're worst fears happened, I bet you would still live to see another day. You see even if you do have genuine concerns, the best way to deal with most situations (unless your physical life is in danger), is to get out of reactive mind and into creative mind. You will sort out your problems more quickly and more effectively if you do.

So really, it's a no brainer. On the one side you have a life of stress, anxiety and despair, and you make ineffective decisions slowly. On the other side you have peace and calm in the here and now with your problems in process of being resolved efficiently and effectively. I know you will say, 'but it's different for me', and you know you might be right. All I know is that when my clients actually get round to solving their problems, they do it in creative mind, not reactive mind. It's just that some clients take a long time before they realize this, and others don't.

So how do you provide alternatives to reactive mind? Well in CBT there are two basic methods:

CBT Method 1 –

Identify the thinking habit then think of a realistic alternative thought that does not involve the thinking habit.

So the other day I thought, "My friend really disrespects me by not returning my texts".

Of course I'm catastrophizing. So someone doesn't return my texts, that doesn't mean I have to jump off the deep end! An alternative thought which does not catastrophize might be:

"I'm upset my friend hasn't returned my texts. I'm sure there is a good reason. I just don't know it yet".

The essence of this method is to diagnose the reactive thinking habit that's causing the problem, and reframe the situation so you are not doing it.

CBT Method 2 –

The second method requires you to interrogate the environment and ask yourself if there is any hard evidence that supports your thinking. Hard evidence is the kind that would stand up in a court of law.

Start by being the counsel for the defense and make a list of all the evidence that supports your current version of reality. Once you have done that, be the counsel for the prosecution. Pick holes in your arguments, and bring in any evidence to support another view.

So taking the reality I had the other day regarding the texts, the only evidence I had I was being ignored was that no texts were being returned. This does not mean, of course, that I am being ignored; this is one possibility, but there may be others. Like she has been rushed into hospital. I simply did not know for sure.

Think about this. Would you want to spend a prison sentence based on the belief you had that the texts were being ignored, or on actual evidence that the texts were being ignored? I bet you would go for the latter. In this case if I were the judge, it would be case dismissed. There is simply no evidence that I am being ignored.

In fact I feel pretty silly for having catastrophized in the way I did. But at the time it felt so compelling. I was angry **because** I was being ignored. That was my reality even though, when we reflect from a more relaxed and creative point of view, there actually is no evidence to support it. I'm now much freer to think up a new, more balanced reality.

Now nobody is suggesting doing this once or twice will solve all your problems. What most people find is that doing it will take the sting out of the tale when you are really digging yourself a hole of stress, anxiety or depression. Where these techniques are really beneficial is over the long term. You will start to notice the patterns of your unhelpful thinking, and get more skilled at finding your way out of it. Eventually, the whole process will become automatic. Therein lies freedom.

In The Enlightenment Plan, I will invite you to keep a record of all the things that distress you. I will then invite you to practice mindfulness or a meditation. This gets you out of the reactive mind to some extent. Then you review the record with a view to spotting the unhelpful reactive thinking habits you were using, and look for evidence to support and contradict your version of reality. I invite you to do this on the form you can download from philtyson.com/downloads. There is even a video to talk you through it.

It's up to you if you use this form or devise your own. I also recommend some books in the 'further reading' section that go into these techniques in a lot more detail.

What is unique about my method is that I'm combining the heart of cognitive behavioral therapy, the wisdom of the modern age, with mindfulness and meditation, the wisdom from the axial age. Both are highly effective and scientifically proven self-development tools. Putting them together means you stand the best chance of success.

This brings us to the end of considering the negative reactive mind habits. It's time now to delve into developing your capacity for creative mind, with meditation and mindfulness.

5.
The Stress Buster Meditation.

There is a story that has been passed around for some time. I've heard it retold by several people, and it goes something like this: A man gets thrown overboard and is in danger of drowning. In desperation he prays to God. A little while later, a lifeboat arrives, but he sends them away saying he had no need of it as God was going to help him. Some time later, a helicopter flew overhead, but he sends them away also, saying he had no need of it as God was going to help him. Later still, a small fishing boat sails past, but he also sent it away, saying he had no need of it as God was going to help him. Well eventually the man drowned, and when he had his audience with the Almighty he was furious with Him that He had not come to his rescue. "Why, after I prayed to you for help, did you not help me?", the man pleaded at God's side.
God responded with, "I sent you a lifeboat, I sent you a helicopter, and I sent you a fishing boat, what more did you expect me to do!"

Many years ago when I was 18 and had just left home, I started to suffer with anxiety and depression. I was having difficulty making the transition from the world of school to the world of work. An older friend was also experiencing depression and anxiety at the same time but for different reasons, and we had both been referred to the same clinical psychology unit.

My friend was prescribed a simple body relaxation meditation of the kind I am going to describe to you. She said it had transformed her life. At the time I thought her problems couldn't have been as severe as mine for such a simple technique to have such remarkable effects. I was convinced my problems were much deeper, requiring lengthy skilled psychotherapy. My friend's symptoms were relieved within six weeks. I, however, continued my search for the solution with intense psychotherapy for another fifteen or so years before discovering the transformative effect of a simple body based meditation of the kind I am going to teach you!

I was like the man who was praying to God. I had a preconceived idea of what the solution to my problems would look like. As a result, I rejected the thing that actually would have been of most help: simply learning to relax.

I see this with my clients all the time. When I describe the basics of good mental health, they listen politely, but disregard them. Like me, they have a preconceived idea of what the solution to their difficulties should look like. For those who are stressed, it's working through their difficulties until they get to a point where they then can stop working so hard. For the anxious, it can be a variety of outcomes, but usually it is to be no longer scared by the things, people and places that have scared them. For the depressed, it is somehow working through the pain of their past, or finding a future they can feel inspired by.

All of these things may indeed help, but not half as effectively if the basics of good mental health are in place. So what are the basics of good mental health?

Well if you recall at the start of this book, I made a list of things I was going to try and achieve while I was writing in Tunisia. They were basically the things you need for good mental health. I'll go through them all in turn.

1. **Drink plenty of water.**

    The body is largely made up of water, and it is essential for efficient operation that it be kept well hydrated. The brain holds a greater proportion of water by mass than any other organ of the body. If you want your brain to work efficiently, you need to drink a minimum of two liters of water every day. For most people, if you wait until you feel thirsty before you drink water, you are already dehydrated.

    Water also flushes toxins out of your body. If you are stressed, anxious or depressed, the chances are your body is producing a lot of the hormones of the fight and flight response; adrenalin and noradrenalin. In large amounts these hormones can give us a 'wired' and 'flu like' feeling, so it's important to drink lots of water to flush them out to help us feel better.

    As you will see below, drinks containing caffeine such as tea, coffee and soda are bad for you if you have stress, anxiety and depression, but they are also diuretics, which mean they work to remove water from your body. The two liters of water I mentioned before should be pure water. Do not include in this any tea, coffee or soda. Filtered water is best to avoid unhelpful and unhealthy additives that are often put in tap water these days. I recently bought and fitted a reverse osmosis filter system for my tap water. Even though I have never plumbed anything in my life, fitting it was easy, even for me.

2. **Avoid Caffeine.**

Tea, coffee and soda all usually contain caffeine, as do some over the counter medicines. Sometimes people with low energy are tempted to take high-energy drinks or 'wake up' pills to give them energy. These mainly rely on sugar and caffeine (in large quantities) to give you a hit and 'boost' your energy.

Caffeine should be avoided if you are stressed, anxious or depressed, simply because caffeine can make your symptoms worse, or even cause them in the first place. In one study of patients who were experiencing panic attacks, an intense form of anxiety where the person often feels like they are about to die, the patients were randomly assigned to a treatment as usual group, or to a no caffeine group. Remarkably the no caffeine group showed a reduction in the number of panic attacks to zero[2]. What this tells me is that more of the symptoms of stress and anxiety can be attributed to caffeine then ever we thought possible. So much so that when I work with someone who has intense anxiety or stress, I try to help

---

2 Panic disorder and social anxiety disorder subtypes in a caffeine challenge test Nardi AE, Lopes FL, Freire RC, Veras AB, Nascimento I, Valença AM, de-Melo-Neto VL, Soares-Filho GL, King AL, Araújo DM, Mezzasalma MA, Rassi A, Zin WA. Psychiatry Res. 2009 Sep 30;169(2):149-53.

him or her to reduce caffeine before I try anything more 'sophisticated'.

There is a rub here though. Suddenly reducing caffeine below what your body is used to can cause anxiety symptoms and depression as well, so it is advisable to reduce your tea, coffee, soda and energy boost products slowly over several weeks. Start with cutting out all caffeine after 6 pm, and work the time back slowly from there.

If you like your tea and coffee, try the decaffeinated brands, which actually taste quite good these days.

3. **Avoid Drugs and Alcohol.**

Many people, for understandable reasons, turn to street drugs and alcohol to help them cope with stress, anxiety and depression. I had one friend who described alcohol as 'relaxation in a bottle'. Some people also use marijuana and other drugs to help them unwind.

When I was working as a university lecturer and experiencing stress, I turned to alcohol and marijuana to help me cope. Pretty quickly I became reliant on these substances to help me unwind at night. Many of my clients also try to cope with their symptoms using these substances, so I know from their experiences, and my own, they can be really difficult to cut back.

The trouble with alcohol is it may relieve your stress, anxiety or depression when you drink it, but it disrupts your body's ability to rest and recuperate, plus making you feel lousy in the morning. For many people a hangover just intensifies their symptoms of anxiety the next day, and sometimes for days afterwards.

Like alcohol, marijuana can also induce anxiety and depression symptoms in some people. My concern with marijuana is that it stays in the body for so long, even when you have stopped smoking it. If you are going to beat your stress, anxiety or depression, you are going to need all your resources to pay attention to, and defeat, your symptoms. You simply cannot do this if you are smoking dope all the time, as for days afterwards, you're not at full awareness.

Like caffeine, if you are going to cut down or eliminate drugs and alcohol, try and do it slowly. Start with cutting out some or all of your intake midweek, when you are working. Then try cutting down at weekends, particularly Sunday evenings when you are at work the next day. When you have managed this, try cutting it out for a full two weeks, you'll be amazed at how much better you will feel. To prove it, use the Tyson Emotional Distress Scale (TEDS) to measure your levels of symptoms, before and after your two weeks. You can download it from philtyson.com/downloads. This should give you the evidence, and the motivation, you need to stop drugs and alcohol altogether, or at least until you start to feel better.

4. **Exercise regularly.**

In Western societies, following the French philosopher Descartes, we tend to separate the mind from the body, and see them as distinct entities. We are then left with the thorny problem of how the mind and the body interact, which has vexed many of the philosophers of mind ever since.

My position is that the notions of 'mind' and 'body' can be useful, some of the time, to describe some of the things we want to talk about. Mind and body, however, are deeply implied by each other, and are no more separate than the sea is from the waves. Similarly sometimes it's useful to talk about 'the sea', and sometimes it's possible to talk about 'the waves', but no separation of the waves from the sea is implied. Sometimes it's useful to talk about 'mind', and sometimes it's useful to talk about 'body' but no separation need be implied.

What this means is that the healthier your body is, the healthier your mind will be too. Some studies have reported that 150 minutes of vigorous physical exercise a week over 8 weeks is just as effective as either antidepressants or cognitive behavioral therapy to beat depression. The jury is still out, however, as not all studies show a robust effect[3]. In my experience stress and anxiety respond particularly well to exercise. If you're stressed, try a boxing class, which seems to be about the best. If you're anxious, I would go with a rhythmic activity, like jogging or swimming, as they seem to be the best for that. If you have not exercised for a while, start simple, just go for a brisk five-minute walk, then steadily increase every day from that. There are also great apps for smart phones these days. On this writing retreat I'm using 'Couch to 5k', a jogging app for iPhone which is a great motivator.

---

3 Nauert, R. (2013). Exercise Can Ease Depression, But More Research Needed. Psych Central. Retrieved on April 29, 2014, from http://psychcentral.com/news/2013/09/13/exercise-can-ease-depression-but-more-research-needed/59483.html

5. **Eat Healthy, Light Foods.**

The relationship between diet and emotional health has been well documented for years now. If you're still eating a lot of junk or processed food, and you are feeling bad, I can't recommend anything better than seeing 'Supersize Me', starring and by Morgan Sturlock. In this documentary a fit and healthy adult male ate junk food for a month, and it nearly killed him! What's most important from our point of view is the change in his mental health: he became depressed, anxious and suffered erratic mood swings.

Everything that is good for your body is also good for your mind. Eat lots of fresh fruit and vegetables. Avoid meat as much as possible, but if you do eat meat, stick to seafood or perhaps a little chicken. Heavy meats like beef, lamb and pork take a long time to digest and create a sluggish feeling in those who eat them. Not the sort of thing you want to eat if you are already feeling low energy.

6. **Do Some Fun Activities.**

When I talk with my stressed, anxious and depressed clients, I am often struck by how bleak their lives sometimes seem from the outside. There is very little joy, and this is mainly because the fun things have been squeezed out by the stress, worry or depression.

There has been a lot of work done over the years to work out what is the best advice to give someone who is depressed. It turns out that behavioral reactivation, or slowly reintroducing fun and enjoyable things to a person's life, is one of the most effective and quickest way to lift someone's mood.[4] In a way, it's common sense. Sitting around ruminating is not going to help anybody, whereas going out with friends and having some fun, even if you don't feel like it, just might lift someone's mood.

If your head is spinning and you're thinking you'll never be able to make all these changes straight off, then that's OK. Just as I did when I arrived for this writing retreat, I set a direction in which I wanted to travel. If you noticed, I set out to do all the things on the list above. It doesn't matter that I haven't done everything on my list; I'll get there in the end. But I have done some of them. Whenever we are making changes in our life it is important to be realistic about what we can achieve. We also need to be kind to ourselves. Just start by adding or removing the easiest thing on the list. When you have done that, and it has become a new habit, start to tackle the next thing on your list. Remember to give yourself a pat on the back for every achievement, however small.

So it's time to check in again. I have been overwhelmed with exhaustion today. After breakfast this morning I returned to my room. The bed held a magnetic attraction for me and I was seduced into a deep sleep. After lunch the same. The bed drew me toward it, and within moments I was carried away into another deep sleep.

I have had similar experiences on retreat before. At some point, usually after two or three days, the space of the new way of life allows a deep and profound rest to emerge from within my being.

[4] Sturmy, P. Behavioral Activation Is an Evidence-Based Treatment for Depression Behav Modif November 2009 33: 818-829

The trick is to be compassionate to myself, and allow it to happen.

Of course there is always a balance to be had between making progress by doing stuff, and just being, in whatever shape that 'being' needs to be taken. In our everyday lives, and especially if we are consumed with stress, anxiety and depression, the balance seems to be too far toward the making progress side of the equation. More to the point, we seem to obsess over the failure to make sufficient progress. In truth, the art of life is in finding the balance. But my experience has always been this is always a work in progress. I never seem to quite get there. But this is OK. Being aware a balance has to be struck and trying to achieve it is a much healthier place than thinking you can do ... do ... do ... *all the time*.

What is at issue here, of course, is a compassionate regard for myself. If I need to rest, I should rest. If I need to work, I should work. But how should these competing needs be balanced in loving regard for my overall wellbeing? The beauty of retreat is that there are no distractions to take me from this task in hand. There is no television, internet, nightclub or bar. There is just me, and this dilemma of being and doing. Even here though, finding the balance is not straightforward.

Meditation also Starts with the Body.

Just as sound mental health starts with looking after the body, so does meditation and mindfulness. But surely mindfulness and meditation is a mental thing, not a body thing? Well if you hold this conception, then you would be wrong. We meditate every bit as much with our body as with our mind, and if you think about it, it becomes obvious. How could we possibly quieten and still our mind if our body is in motion? So we must first learn to still the body.

Through the ages, the classic way this has been done is with a variety of body meditations. As this is a book about stress, anxiety and depression, I am going to teach you a meditation in active progressive muscular relaxation. This is the exercise my friend was taught when I was eighteen, and from which she gained so much relief, and is excellent for stress and anxiety. I call it the 'Stress Buster', and give a copy to most of my stressed, anxious or depressed clients at the end of the first session.

In order to understand the reason why I do this and why I want you to start with this meditation, it will first require us to contemplate again the nature of our crazy modern world, and the nature of stress, anxiety and depression.

In Chapter 1 I talked about a paradox in the world we live. On the one hand, most of our demons are of our own making. We fret about the perceived slights of other people, we worry about things that have never happened, and probably will never happen (studies show that over 95% of worries never come true), and we get lost in a lack of meaning and purpose. All these threats are self-generated.

Yet at the same time, we live in a world that does not meet our human needs. Our lives are so full of stuff, we have insufficient time to look after our bodies. Our working lives, and increasingly our spare time (with the internet and computer gaming), is caught in the headlights of mental stuff to do. We are becoming more and more creatures of the mind. Furthermore, the thing we need to ground us in reality, an extended network of stable social and family relationships, is becoming more and more inaccessible.

As our head, and the mental stuff we need to do with it, get fuller and fuller, we become more and more estranged from our bodies; it is as if they are of secondary importance. Judging by the epidemic rates of obesity in children and adults, it looks like whole armies within the population have completely lost touch with their bodies and what they might need to thrive and be healthy. New generations are the first in history with a predicted lower life expectancy than their parents.

As we become lost in our mental world, however, the pains of our bodies remain unacknowledged. Stress is not just a mental phenomenon; we feel stress in the body too. Our muscles tighten in response to it. Our stomachs secrete acid and create discomfort in response to it. And our bowels react with irregularity in response to it.

Anxiety states and depressions are no less felt in the body. Anxiety, being fear, sets in motion a torrent of psychophysiological changes that severely disrupt the healthy working of the body. Depression brings about a withdrawal and lethargy that undermine physical fitness, and our ability to respond vigorously to the challenges of life. One day of bed rest causes a loss of muscle strength of 4%.

The discipline of psychoneuroimmunology, which looks at the relationship between our emotional and mental wellbeing, the nervous system, the endocrine system and the immune system, is revealing with glaring scientific starkness that our poor mental health causes poor physical health. To emphasize once more, from cancer to Crohn's disease and arthritis to diabetes, the stresses, anxieties and depressions of our sophisticated modern world are killing us. They may be killing us slowly, but they are killing us none the less.

So there is a link between our mental states and our body states. Body meditations help us to become more mindful of that connection, and in calming the body, we come to calm the mind also.

The 'Stress Buster' Active Progressive Muscular Relaxation Meditation.

For this meditation you need to lie flat on a bed or on the floor with your head supported and your arms by your side. As with all meditations, your body temperature will drop slightly, so prepare by wearing appropriate loose clothing, or cover yourself with a blanket.

You can do this meditation in one of two ways. You can listen to a recording by downloading it from philtyson.com/downloads. I have a range to choose from including some with music and binaural beats.

You don't need a recording of course; you can just as effectively follow the instructions below.

In this meditation you should apply the following procedure to every part of your body.

1. Breathe in and hold it.
2. Tense a part of your body.
3. Notice the tension in that part of your body.
4. Breathe out, relaxing that part of the body.

I find the following order to be helpful.
1. Right foot by pulling your toes back.
2. Left foot by pulling your toes back.

3. Right lower leg.
4. Left lower leg.
5. Right upper leg.
6. Left upper leg.
7. Buttocks.
8. Lower back by arching gently.
9. Stomach.
10. Upper back and shoulders by raising your shoulders to your ear.
11. Eyes and mouth.
12. Nose.
13. Any remaining area(s) of tension.

After you have gone through this routine, you may wish to spend a few moments to several minutes enjoying the feeling of relaxation it brings.

If you go through the whole routine once, it should take about 5 minutes. If you want to make the meditation longer, repeat each step twice or three times.

Warning: If you have muscular skeletal or joint problems, you may find the tensing parts of this exercise uncomfortable. You can still do the exercise but omit the instructions to tense your muscles.

What can I expect doing this meditation?

It is important to remember that the benefits of meditation come by the frequency and consistency of practice. The 10 week Enlightenment Plan starts you off with just five minutes a day for the first week. This is just enough to get you started and work out how you are going to fit meditation into your routine. Please look at Week 1 in the Appendix for more detailed instructions.

Coping with Your Wandering Mind.

When you start meditating, the first thing that virtually everybody notices is that his or her mind wanders. One minute you are tensing and relaxing your leg, then the next thing you realize you have been doing the shopping list and had completely forgotten that you were supposed to be doing the meditation.

I cannot emphasize this enough. This is perfectly normal.

Indeed whether this is your first meditation or your 5000th, it is still perfectly normal.

When we set our mind to focus on something, in this case the tension in our muscles, we cannot fail to be distracted. People respond to this in a range of predictable ways.

1. **They think they are doing something wrong.** No you are not doing anything wrong, it is the nature of meditation that your mind wanders. What is important is that you celebrate that you have noticed, give yourself a little 'yay', and gently bring your attention back to the meditation.
2. **People think that the meditation is better the less you get distracted.** As you get more practiced with meditation things do change, but it is important to realize that all the time you spend in meditation is equally valuable, whether you are more or less distracted.
3. **People try to force it.** If you try too hard to keep the object of

the meditation in mind, it is counter productive. There is no point doing the meditation in a way that gives you stress. Your mind will wander. Just get over it. Hold this fact lightly, with a sense of equanimity and compassion, that is the key.

That should be enough to get you started. You can either continue reading about the other meditations, or if you are keen to start practicing, go straight to The Enlightenment Plan Week 1 in the Appendix. If you do get started now, come straight back. You will need to keep reading to get the best out of the plan.

How to Vary This Meditation.

This meditation is great if you are holding a lot of tension in your body due to stress, anxiety or depression. That's why I am recommending it. Sometimes you may not be in a position to tense and relax your muscles, say if you are on a train or in a meeting or simply because you want to try something more subtle. If this is the case, simply breathe in, allow your attention to wander over the right foot, notice any tension within the foot, then as you breathe out imagine your right foot relaxing. Continue with the next part of your body as before. Doing this without deliberately tensing your muscles is known as a 'body scan' meditation.

6.
The Mindfulness of Breathing Meditation.

I feel an apprehension about writing this chapter, and it has been building for the last two days. The apprehension concerns how important the mindfulness of breathing is in the history and practice of meditation, and a feeling of inadequacy to do it justice. This morning, after breakfast, the unease deepened. Part of me wanted to go to the gym to help relieve the ache in my shoulder that has developed from being hunched over a computer all week. Part of me wanted to read my book. Part of me wanted to sleep. Part of me wanted to start writing.

I am caught up, in other words, in the incessant ramblings of my mind. Those ramblings I'm experiencing as a feeling of dissatisfaction, unease and inadequacy: in other words, pain. My energies are split, conflicted and the present moment is unsatisfactory because I'm caught in a range of future unsatisfactory possibilities. I'm living in the future, albeit the immediate future. I'm not living in the here and now.

It's remarkable, but it is just these kinds of mental and emotional turmoil that the mindfulness of breathing is so adept at helping to resolve. In order to explain this I will first describe the practice, and you will then be better able to imagine why it has its powerful, transformative effect.

The Mindfulness of Breathing Practice.

This practice is in four stages. Before you start you need to be in the right posture. Traditionally the posture used for meditation has been the full or half lotus position, or alternatively to sit legs straddled across a large firm cushion. My experience of trying these postures was typical of western adults. It was painful. So painful in fact it became a distinct obstacle to learning to meditate.

I don't want you to suffer the same pain and distraction. I recommend therefore you try the following posture:

Sit on a dining chair with the back two feet slightly raised with an inch block of wood. This helps to tilt your spine slightly. It is important to keep your spine straight and not slouched in the chair, so position a firm cushion behind the base of your back. To prevent your shoulders rounding and becoming uncomfortable over time, rest your hands on a large cushion placed on your lap.

This posture will give you everything you need to remain relaxed, but alert and stable. By all means feel free to try the more traditional postures, but wait until you have finished The Enlightenment Plan. That way you will have given yourself the best chance of learning meditation without feeling any discomfort.

So moving on to the practice itself.

This practice, as the name suggests, is based around becoming aware of your breath. All meditations require you to focus your attention on something. In the last one it was your body. In this one it will be the in flow and out flow of your breath.

Variations on the mindfulness of breathing have been practiced across all religious and philosophical traditions, probably going back three thousand years at least. It must, therefore, have benefited literally billions of individuals over that time. The breath is an ideal object of focus because in calming the breath, it has a naturally calming effect on the mind. Not only that, it is immensely practical. We all breathe, all the time. We therefore take it with us into every situation we face, including the stressful ones. So the mindfulness of breathing is always available to us, whenever we need to turn to it for help.

You can do this meditation in one of two ways. You can listen to a recording by downloading one from philtyson.com/downloads. I have a range to choose from including some with music and binaural beats.

You don't need a recording of course; you can just as effectively follow the instructions below.

Stage One.

Find yourself in an alert and upright meditation posture of the kind I just described.

Start by taking a few moments to become aware of your body. Do a mini body scan of the kind I described at the end of the previous chapter.

When you feel you have 'arrived', gently become aware of your breath.

It is important not to change the speed of your breath. Your breath may be short or it may be long. It may even turn into a yawn. It doesn't matter. The crucial thing is to be an observer of the breath in whatever shape and direction it takes, not its controller.

When you have got into a pattern of observation, start counting your breathing at the end of the out breath.

Breath in … breath out … 1

Breath in … breath out … 2, etc.

Pay attention to that very subtle moment when your lungs are completely empty before counting. The more you pay attention to this subtle point at the end of the out breath, the more effective will be your meditation.

Count the out breaths until you get to ten, and then start again from one.

Of course, as in the previous meditation, your mind will wander. This is normal and perfectly acceptable. When you notice your mind has wandered off, congratulate yourself for becoming aware, and pay attention to your breathing again, and start counting from 1. As Eckhart Tolle once wrote, "The moment you realize you are not present, you are present".

When you are ready move on to stage two.

Stage 2.

In this stage, we still pay attention to the natural and unforced inflow and outflow of the breath, but we pay particular attention to the beginning of the in breath, the moment when the lungs are just starting to fill.

This is almost the same point as in stage 1, so it is a very subtle difference, and you need to pay very careful attention.

Start counting the in breaths from 1 to 10 as before. When you get to 10 start counting again from 1.

In some ways the transition from stage 1 to stage 2 is representative of the kind of change we want to cultivate in meditation - from reacting to the mind, to anticipating it.

If you are new to the mindfulness of breathing, I would just concentrate on these two stages for at least a week before moving on to the next two stages. This is what we do in The Enlightenment Plan.

Stage 3.

In this stage, hopefully your mind will have become sufficiently settled to be able to drop the counting and still remain focused in the present.

Again pay attention to the natural inflow and outflow of the breath. Focus in particular on the rise and fall of the chest, and the sensations this causes.

My experience of this stage is that even if I was able to hold my attention when counting, my mind invariably starts to wander without the counting to anchor it. Treat your wandering mind with kindness and equanimity. We are not trying to get anywhere, and holding your attention or not holding your attention makes no difference to the long-term benefits of meditation. If you are naturally a perfectionist, this gives you a great opportunity to practice being 'good enough'.

When you are ready, move on to stage 4.

Stage 4.

This is the subtlest stage of all; so don't worry if initially you find it hard. It can take several weeks to get the hang of it.

As with stage 3, observe the natural inflow and outflow of your breath without counting.

This time pay particular attention to the sensation of the breath as it passes in and out through the tip of your nose.

Remember this is a very subtle sensation, but you will get the hang of it with practice.

The Benefits of the Mindfulness of Breathing.

At the start of the book I invited you to imagine me locked in the back of a police van. Continuing the story, they drove me to Wythenshaw hospital, a large municipal hospital complex in South Manchester. Their Accident and Emergency department is equipped to handle 'psychiatric emergencies'. Apparently the police had detained me under the provisions of the Mental Health Act, which meant I had to be interviewed by a psychiatrist and a social worker. It was they who would decide what would happen to me next.

You can imagine my distress. One moment I was in such a desperately low place I was using a knife to end my life. The next I'm being bundled into the back of a police van. And now, what seemed like only minutes later, I had to account for myself to two strangers, blood dripping down my wrist and onto the hospital floor.

I told them everything.

The psychiatrist and social worker retreated to consider their verdict. About half an hour later they returned, "We think you should go and visit your mum for the weekend".

That was it! I was incredulous, and I flew into a rage.

"Is that the sum total of your combined professional expertise, go and visit your mum!"

"What do I need to say to get out of here", I barked at the police officer who was, by that time, restraining me.

At that point I knew that no one could help me. If I wanted to get out of this depression I had to take responsibility for what was going through my mind. It was me who had to find the solution. I knew that now.

I enrolled on a six-week mindfulness of breathing meditation course. It gave me the tools to take my life back.

I can't say the following months were easy, far from it, but I threw myself into the practice. Every day, sometimes twice a day, I built the capacity of my mind to remain focused. You see with stress, anxiety and depression, your mind's energies become scattered and unfocussed. Quickly the mind is trying to do too many things, and you become overwhelmed and demoralized.

For me, the mindfulness of breathing had a great integrating effect. It is as if, simply by doing the practice, all the problems I was dwelling on seem to recede. Often, by the end of the practice, I had formed a clear plan of what I needed to do next. All without really trying.

As the weeks turned into months my depression started to lift. Life was still hard. I was, after all, still at rock bottom. But I steadily made progress. I went for my first retreat after four months, which deepened my practice considerably. It gave me a vision of the peace of what life could be like. The veil was starting to lift. Within a year I had been meditating every day, I had been on three retreats, built up my physical fitness, and was starting to withdraw from my meds. The rest, as they say, is history.

Why is Meditation so Effective?

Why, given I had trained in psychology and psychotherapy, had had 7 years of therapy myself, and eaten heaven knows how many psychiatric meds, had these strategies not worked, but meditation had? Don't get me wrong, all those things helped to a point, but they didn't offer me the ultimate cure I was looking for.

Well it can't be underestimated how important it was to realize that, in the end, I had to help myself. I had looked for the cure in the eyes of other people. In the end I had to look into myself, and stop the incessant worry, anxiety and depression by changing what I paid attention to.

I learnt the hard way, that ultimately paying attention to the problems of my life had given them the energy they needed to be sustained. I had to create a new life, and simply leave the problems behind.

Of course our problems are central to who we are. I would tell anybody who would listen just how bad my childhood was! If I were to be happy, I was going to have to leave that story and that self behind. But what would be left of me if I simply dropped the pain and the struggle. Perhaps in the back of the police van, I found the courage to see. To dare to walk a different path.

What of meditation? Clearly the meditation was instrumental in giving me the skills to do this. So how does meditation work? Despite the years of research on meditation, all we can really say from a scientific point of view is that it does work. As to the why, that is still deeply mysterious. Here are some of the things we do know. These are research findings that particularly caught my eye, and are not meant to be some kind of scholarly summary.

Meditation Builds 'Happier' Brains.

For many years it was thought that the human brain could not change after early adulthood. We now know this is not true. Indeed new brain cells form right into old age, and even when close to death.

Brain scans comparing long-term experienced meditators show the areas of the brain concerned with happiness, including the left frontal regions, are increased in activation.[5]

It appears to show that meditation literally changes the architecture of the brain, building our capacity to experience joy.

Meditation Builds More Integrated Brains.

I suggested earlier that the mindfulness of breathing meditation could help to integrate and harmonize our minds when we are being pulled in two or more directions. Research looking at brain waves shows that this integration also reveals itself in a more integrated pattern of brain waves in experienced meditators.[6]

Meditation Prevents Relapse in Depression.

I've already discussed this finding but it is worth repeating. In people who have experienced several episodes of depression, the one factor that is likely to 'rekindle' a further episode is rumination. Becoming more mindful of our mental state by practicing mindfulness techniques and meditation can help prevent rumination and so cut depression relapse.[7]

---

[5] see Davidson, R.J. (2004) Well-being and affective style: Neural substrates and biobehavioural correlates. Philosophical Transactions of the Royal Society. 359:1395-1411.

[6] Lutz, A. L. Greischar, N. Rawlings, M. Ricard, and R Davidson (2004) Long-term meditators self-induce high-amplitude gama synchrony during mental practice. Proceedings of the National Academy of Sciences 101:16369-16373.

[7] Zindel V. Segal, J. Mark G. Williams, and John D. Teasdale (2002) Mindfulness-Based Cognitive Therapy for Depression: A New Approach to Preventing Relapse. Guilford Press.

Mindfulness and Meditation Prevents Combat Stress in Soldiers.

In a study that taught mindfulness techniques to combat soldiers before their tour of duty, it was found that simply by being able to pay more attention to the difficulties of their combat role, it helped soldiers cope well with their job while on their tour of duty, and helped prevent posttraumatic stress disorder upon their return.[8]

This is an interesting finding because our instinct when things get really bad is to not pay attention and dissociate from what is happening. What this study shows is that this may not only make things worse in the short term, but may also lead to unhealthy processing of the traumatic events causing post traumatic stress disorder later.

What these, and the voluminous other studies show, is that mindfulness and meditation promote positive mental health and wellbeing. However, it doesn't say why it does. The way I explain it to my clients is that meditation is a little bit like working out at the gym. If I exercise my muscles they get stronger as a consequence. This means I am able to work more efficiently, lift heavier objects and suffer less injury in my every day life. Similarly with meditation. By 'exercising' our capacity to pay attention to the here and the now, we build our ability and capacity to do so. The more we can then live in the now, rather than ruminate about the past or the future, the happier we become. But this is a skill. And practice makes perfect. This is what I believe, and it makes sense to me. But like I say, no one really knows for sure why it works.

---

8 See http://happinessbeyondthought.blogspot.co.uk/2013/01/mindfulness-training-for-marinesnew.html

The Secret of Meditation: Acceptance and Compassion.

I was on a Buddhist retreat once. At dinner I was at a table with two experienced Buddhists and I listened, but did not take part, in their conversation. They were experienced Buddhists because both of them had adopted Buddhist names which, in this particular tradition, meant they had gone through a long process of ordination. They were reflecting on the death of a fellow Buddhist, and were sad that he had not reached enlightenment before his passing. Their attention then turned to their own enlightenment. In view of the death of their friend, they were intent on redoubling their efforts in meditation. If they worked hard enough, they were sure they would be successful, and eventually reach enlightenment before they died.

For me, enlightenment is not something to be achieved in the future, it's something to discover in the present. What I was more concerned about with these two individuals, however, was the view that somehow enlightenment was something they had to work hard at. This didn't feel very compassionate for them. Rather it felt to me like a macho endurance race (they were both men). Nothing, it seemed to me, could be further from enlightenment than this.

The practices of meditation, whichever ones you choose, provide the first ingredient you need to wake up from your stress, anxiety or depression. Meditation practices remind you to be in the present moment: in the now. Peace, contentment and happiness are qualities that can only ever be experienced right now. Think about it, have you ever experienced tomorrow's happiness today? Of course this is absurd. We can only wake up from our pain into something more creative right now. Indeed, we have everything we need to be happy, right now. If we are not happy right now, this is because our mind is creating trouble for us. Meditation calms the mind, and allows us to connect with the peace and contentment that was always there, but just couldn't be seen. Unfortunately by conceptualizing enlightenment as something to be found in the future, these Buddhists were probably destined never to find it.

Meditation, however, needs a couple more ingredients to be effective. I have alluded to them already, but for the sake of clarity, I want to make them explicit now.

The first is the acceptance of what is. In meditation you will have a whole range of experiences. Some days you will find it really difficult to practice, other days it will come more easily. It is easy to let our unhelpful mind turn these into 'failures' and 'successes'. In the judgment we make a fatal error: we fail to accept our experience in meditation just as it is. By making a judgment, we drop out of the here and now and into a mind narrative comparing our current experience with an idea of what we think our experience should be. This will create a feeling of discontent, perhaps even anger. Then, of course, realizing what we are doing, we might start judging ourselves for having made a judgment, and we could easily dig our hole of unhappiness even deeper.

Whenever you realize you have fallen away from the here and now and into a mind trap like this, or any other, simply accept what you have done ... pat yourself on the back for waking up to it, and return to the meditation practice undisturbed.

The two Buddhists I was describing before were not very accepting of where they were right now. For them, they were not enlightened, and the desired state was to be enlightened. It seemed to me they couldn't help but cause themselves pain.

The second quality you will need to cultivate when practicing meditation is compassion for yourself. If you find yourself in an uncomfortable posture, or if upsetting thoughts and feelings come to you in meditation, treat yourself with kindness and compassion. Yes accept that this is your experience right now, but give the experience space just to be with kindness. Again, the macho approach of the two Buddhists I listened to didn't seem to be very compassionate to themselves. In fact they sounded like they were creating a rod for their own back.

Meditation, then, could be summarized like this: A practice that keeps you in the here and now that you cultivate with an acceptance of what is and with compassion.

I don't underestimate how difficult this might be for some of you. I worked with one client, a young man, whose parents had been very critical of him. Not surprisingly he was now very critical of himself. He reported to me that whenever he tried to be accepting and compassionate toward himself in mediation it made him cry. Fortunately the next practice, the loving kindness meditation, is designed to help you build acceptance and compassion not only for yourself, but other people as well.

Imagine, though, what life would be like, if you could accept more of the good and the bad life throws at you, without having to get into some kind of battle with it. Imagine also being more able to extend kindness and compassion to yourself, especially when you feel pain. The meditation and mindfulness techniques I am teaching you will give you that ability, as they have given many others before you. They certainly did for me.

It's now about 7.00 pm on day six. I'm really pleased with my progress. I've got to this point, which is about 2/3 of the way already. Emotionally I'm starting to settle into the experience. I have managed the gym today, and I've only had three gin and tonics all week, which is great restraint for me.

I now feel I am well behind what I've come to call 'text-gate'. Looking back I clearly became completely absorbed in what was, after all, a trivial thing. This, of course, is what life is like for me some of the time, and for my clients, most of the time. We overreact to event after event in our lives creating untold unnecessary misery for ourselves. Nonetheless, at the time, it feels compelling, 'real', and draws us in as surely as a syringe draws blood from our vein. Two or three upsets like that a week and we quickly start hating our lives.

The trick, of course, is not to get caught in the first place. So what should you do if you do find yourself hooked in with too much stress, anxiety or depression?

The Thinking Form.

The method, which forms the backbone of The Enlightenment Plan, is simple.

First, make a note of all the negative thoughts you have about yourself, your future or the world you live in. You might choose to collect these in real time as you go about your daily life. Write them in the first box of The Thinking Form.

Tip: If you have a lot of 'what if' type thoughts, finish off the 'what if' and put the last thing down you think. For example I might think 'what if my girlfriend leaves me'. If I finish that off I might discover I'm scared I might never find another girlfriend again. So in the box I would put as the thought 'girlfriend leaving and being alone forever'.

Second, rate out of 100 how much you believed each thought <u>when you thought it.</u> 100 is you completely believed it, 0 is you didn't believe it at all.

Third, choose a meditation or mindfulness practice to do. This will help bring you into the present moment with acceptance and compassion. It will also help to get you out of reactive mind and into creative mind, and so be better able to 'read' reality and change.

Fourth, with your frame of mind hopefully softened a little, use the perspective gained to identify which unhelpful thinking habits have seduced you into distress.

Fifth, look for evidence that supports the point of view for the most compelling thought we were holding (usually the highest scoring, or 'hot thought'), and look for evidence that contradicts or does not support the view we were holding.

Sixth, create an alternative, more balanced thought, that does not fall into any thinking trap and takes full view of the evidence.

It really is that simple. You can download 'The Thinking Form' to help you collect the information at philtyson.com/downloads. There is also a video with examples to help you fill in the form.
This was the method I used to help get me out of 'text-gate'.

Continuing to reflect the next day: I arrived a week ago today, and I am now half way through this writing and meditation retreat. The night before last I had an evening off. I had a few alcoholic drinks, and thoroughly enjoyed them. Yesterday I reread and touched up all the work I had already done. If you like, it was a sort of staging post before writing the next chapter on loving kindness which I will start presently.

Surprisingly, most of my practice so far has been focused on mindfulness rather than meditation. I have been meditating every day, but my rhythms seem to be just once or twice and only occasionally three times which is not what I had anticipated. I have, however, been enjoying and deepening my mindful awareness, a topic I will discuss in Chapter 8. I have been particularly enjoying mindful eating and mindful walking.

I feel like the workings of my mind have slowed down, and I've become more aware of when my mind is causing me problems, which, in a subtle way, appears to be most of the time. We identify with our mind so completely when we are stressed, anxious and depressed, that we can be shocked when we wake up a little bit to discover we are not our minds. When you practice, you will be amazed to discover your mind thinks you, rather than the other way round!

Mindfulness and meditation gives you the psychological space to observe your mind in real time. So I have been observing all the little ways I judge other people in the hotel. I have been observing all the little ways I create stress for myself.

When you get out of reactive mind, as I believe I have done, you start to see how the mind is like an unruly child. It is always demanding attention, and if it doesn't get it, starts being naughty.

I also started to get what I sometimes call 'sparkles of enlightenment'. It's as if I move, momentarily, into profound presence of now, I start to get insights into the bigger picture of life. Now they are just moments, I'm not claiming to be some guru, and they will come to you too if you follow The Enlightenment Plan diligently.

One occasion, I already mentioned, was the connection I noticed between two spiders on the sand. Another was catching my reflection in the lift mirror and seeing beyond my ageing physical self into something more, well, timeless. The final one was looking out of the balcony and feeling a connection with the palm trees. It was as if I had to say hello to every single one of them so none was left out.

Now I know this sounds crazy. They were just little moments. However, they were moments when I felt a harmony and a connection with the world. Then the veil closed again as quickly as it had opened. But the feeling of wellbeing stayed with me.

My broader life circumstances have also fallen into some sort of perspective. I have come to realize the death of my friend and my relationship issues have hardened me a little inside. I guess this is an understandable reaction to pain. A kind of withdrawal. But actions have consequences. In hardening myself a little to protect myself from pain, I also hardened my responses to other people. This I have been experiencing as intolerance and stress. I now realize, when I return home, I need to focus my attention on being kind to myself and other people. I need to be more accepting of them, and allowing love and compassion to emerge where irritation and stress has existed.

No doubt the loving kindness meditation will help me to do this, and I will turn our attention to that now.

7.

The Loving Kindness Meditation.

Love and kindness are gendered concepts in the West, and especially so in the North of England. Men, so I've been led to believe, are supposed to be strong and fearless, not loving and kind. Some of this, no doubt, stems from the archetypes of man as warrior (strong, fearless) and woman as mother (loving, kind).

Sometimes, though, being a mother requires strength and courage, and sometimes it takes strength and courage to be loving and kind.

More broadly, beyond gender, we have a problem with love and kindness. I think it stems from love and kindness not making good television or movies. It is so much easier to make dramas about hate, treachery and double dealing. The television programs and movies we watch literally program us to be unloving and unkind. Deep down though, it is our true nature to love and to be kind, and our lives are so much happier when we receive love and kindness from others.

In fact science is starting to show that the very fabric of our bodies relies on love and kindness to thrive and be healthy. When we receive love and kindness from others, our body releases a chemical called oxytocin, the so-called 'cuddle hormone'. When it is released it gives us an enormous feeling of wellbeing and connection. Indeed, it helps us to empathize and connect with others.

Scientists are also discovering the oxytocin receptors in just about every place on the body they look. When we give and receive love, it is as if every cell in our body sings and becomes more alive.

Unfortunately the lives we live today, atomized and disconnected from our closest friends and relatives, means that we probably receive less love and kindness now than ever in the history of our species. No wonder many of us feel so mentally and physically sick. Our cells are being starved of oxytocin.

Of course all the major religious traditions knew the transformative power of love. Jesus made love the central message of the Christian faith when he said, "You're your neighbor as yourself". Similarly, love and kindness is at the heart of the Buddhist religion. In fact the Dali Lama once said his religion was "kindness".

Love and kindness are important to cultivate for anyone who is in emotional pain. I say this because love and kindness are the opposite of stress, anxiety and depression. I know this sounds odd, but it is true. It is virtually impossible to feel love and kindness, and at the same time feel stressed, anxious and depressed. I'm not talking, of course, about the neurotic clinging kind of love, but a genuine heartfelt love and care for the world and all the creatures in it. Love and kindness are the epitome of connection. Stress, anxiety and depression can only thrive with disconnection.

If you genuinely want to move away from your stress, anxiety and depression ... learn to love, learn to be kind.

Fortunately there is a meditation practice that, if used regularly, transforms our capacity to give and receive love and kindness. Here's how I used it on this retreat.

If you recall, when I arrived for this writing and meditation retreat, I felt irritated and stressed. I went for what 'should' have been a really nice and relaxing time to try and unwind. I booked a Turkish bath, Jacuzzi and massage. It started well. The Turkish bath itself was really pretty, and I practiced mindfulness by taking in the details of the mosaic tiles. The Jacuzzi bath was like nothing I'd been in before. A room with one large bathtub, filled with water, and when turned on, millions of bubbles cascaded over my body, and I practiced mindfulness by absorbing myself in the energy of the bubbles as they vigorously fought with each other for my attention. I noted how beautiful yet utterly unpredictable they were, and imagined something similar might go on at the level of electrons within matter.

The problem started with the massage. The table was uncomfortable, and as the massage progressed my head and eyes began to ache. I started to wish the massage over. What was worse was on two occasions someone came into the massage room and had a conversation with my therapist. In Phil's world this shouldn't happen. I was angry.

I left decidedly agitated but contained. It stayed with me though, with a mild but steady background rumination. Eventually I started to feel sad.

I went for dinner and couldn't find anybody to get me a soup spoon.

My soup was on my table getting cold. I eventually found a waiter and snapped at him. When he returned with the soup spoon, he didn't look me in the eye. I had intimidated him.

I felt stressed, sad, and now guilty.

As this represented a problem with my emotional response to individuals, I decided to do the loving kindness meditation. As you will discover yourself, I didn't manufacture any artificial or pretend love or kindness toward the waiter I had snapped at. I did however mark an intention, to be loving and kind to him in the future. I did the loving kindness meditation straight after dinner.

The next time we met, he was understandably cautious of me, but I tried to let my good wishes come out in his direction. The next day, he had softened some more; by the third day, he shook my hand, and now we greet each other as if we were old friends. He speaks little English and I speak even less Arabic, but cultivating loving kindness in the meditation helped to soften my attitude to him, and he responded in kind. So I arrived in Tunisia with no one to offer me love and kindness. Now, thanks to my own efforts, I get two mini doses of giving and receiving loving kindness every day. Once at lunch, and once at dinner. It could have been otherwise. I could have sat at the other side of the dinning room and spent two weeks ruminating on the unhelpful waiter.

So what is the loving kindness meditation, and how do you do it?

The loving kindness meditation I will show you is most closely associated with the Buddhist tradition where it is know as the metta bhavana. Metta means loving kindness and bhavana means cultivation. The metta bhavana is one of four meditations, known as 'the heavenly abodes'. The others are the cultivation of compassion, sympathetic joy and equanimity.

As you will have noticed during this book, I have been emphasizing the development of compassion and equanimity in all the meditations, and with the way I'm going to show you, you can bring all of the 'heavenly abodes' into this practice if you like.

The Loving Kindness Meditation.

You can do this meditation in one of two ways. You can listen to a recording by downloading one from the selection at philtyson.com/downloads. I have a range to choose from including one with music and binaural beats.

You don't need a recording of course; you can just as effectively follow the instructions below.

Sit in your meditation posture and start by taking some time to settle into your body by bringing your awareness to it. Like laying firm foundations, if you take the time to settle completely before beginning, you will get more from the practice. When you have settled the body, and 'arrived', take some time to follow the rhythms of your breath. When you feel focused, we can begin.

Stage 1 – Loving kindness for yourself.

In this stage, we turn our attention to ourselves. We often have a complex and sometimes problematic relationships with ourselves, but we are a human being, and like all human beings, we deserve to be happy. Start the practice by reminding yourself of this. You might then repeat the following phrases:

May I be well.
May I be happy.
May I be free from danger.
May my life be easy and comfortable.
May I be successful.

If it helps, you can co-ordinate the phrases with your breath, or follow another rhythm. It is entirely up to you.

It is highly unlikely that your heart will suddenly open to feeling complete and utter love and kindness to yourself. It might, but what is important is that you are stating intent. It is an intention to by loving and kind to yourself, and wish yourself well, etc. As the client I mentioned in an earlier chapter, who cried when starting to wish himself well, you may find a whole range of conflicting emotions pop up. That's completely OK. Just allow those emotions to be there, acknowledge them, and gently return to the practice.

As with all meditations, your mind will do everything it can to sabotage the object of your attention, which, in this case, is your well wishing. When you become aware of your mind having wandered, give yourself a 'yay' for 'waking up', and gently turn your attention back to the practice.

Stage 2 – The Good Friend or Benefactor.

The next stage is to cultivate loving kindness toward someone who has been a good friend or a benefactor to us. The idea is that as we already have a strong memory of good feelings for this person, so we simply remind ourselves of the love and kindness we feel toward them. We might start simply by reminding ourselves that they are a human being, and as such, deserve to be happy and without suffering and pain. As in the previous stage, you might repeat the following phrases while keeping them in your mind's eye:

May you be well.
May you be happy.
May you be free from danger.
May your life be easy and comfortable.
May you be successful.

Stage 3 – The Unfamiliar Person.

Everybody who comes into our life was once unfamiliar to us. How we treat the general category of 'unfamiliar person' is therefore really important. Over the years I have worked with lots of people who are lonely and have few meaningful relationships with others. Often I find that their relationship to the 'unfamiliar' people in their lives reveal the cause of their isolation: They often refuse to engage with unfamiliar people. What this means is no one ever traverses the path from unfamiliar to familiar person, because unfamiliar people are simply ignored.

Unfamiliar people are, however, extremely important to the smooth flow of our lives. We live in a complex, interdependent world. We rely enormously on people we barely, if at all, know: the postman, the person who sells us our newspaper, the person who delivers the milk, or makes us our coffee in the canteen.

This stage of the loving kindness meditation gives us the opportunity to re-evaluate our relationship with unfamiliar people. Choose just one such person in your life for this practice.

We might start simply by reminding ourselves that they are a human being, and as such, deserve to be happy and without suffering and pain. You might then repeat the same phrases as in the previous stages while keeping them in your minds eye:

May you be well.
May you be happy.
May you be free from danger.
May your life be easy and comfortable.
May you be successful.

As we don't know much about this kind of person by definition, it can be a real stretch on the imagination to keep this part of the practice going. I sometimes find it helpful to imagine these people in their social and family contexts. By reminding ourselves that someone loves this person, I find it somehow easier to connect with loving and kind feelings for them.

Stage 4 – The Difficult Person.

In this stage of the meditation we bring to mind someone we are having difficulty with right now. Again the aim is not to cultivate artificial or fabricated emotion. We do have genuine difficulty with this person, and the emotions we feel in relationship to them will no doubt come to the fore.

What is important is our intention to move beyond the current difficulty we have with that person, to see them as a human being. However angry or upset we feel about them right now, we try to connect with their humanity, and understand that they do deserve to be happy. If you are having difficulty accepting even this, try thinking about the friends and family of this person, and how this 'difficult' person being happy might make these other people happy also. Again, repeat the following phrases while keeping this person in your mind's eye:

May you be well.
May you be happy.
May you be free from danger.
May your life be easy and comfortable.
May you be successful.

As our social relationships are complex and continually changing, it is not uncommon for a person who is in the 'good friend' part of the meditation one week, can be found in the 'difficult person' section the next week!

Stage 5 – Equanimity.

In theory at least, all of the people we have meditated on so far are equally deserving of happiness and wellbeing. We might not feel that way though. The final stage of this meditation is to try and even out the good feelings for each of the four people, so no one receives more than the others. There are many ways you could do this, so see what works best for you. I'm quite a visual person, so I imagine the good friend is sitting opposite me with the unfamiliar person to my left and the difficult person to my right.

When you feel you have reached equanimity, or as close as you are going to get, take this well wishing for yourself and others and gradually increase it to include everybody in your street, then your town, then your country, continent until eventually your loving kindness extends to the whole of humanity, without favor. You can also extend it to all living creatures, or indeed, the whole of creation including extraterrestrials if you so choose. But that's up to you.

When you are first learning this meditation, it is a good idea to practice on people who are fairly safe. For this reason the usual advice is to go for people about the same age as you with whom you do not have a sexual relationship. As you will see below, once you are well practiced you can start changing things somewhat, but for the time being, until you are confident in the practice, stay safe.

Important Information: The loving kindness is a profound meditation, and it is tempting to have a go straightaway. Please resist the temptation to do so. This meditation may bring up strong emotions, and you need to have some experience of the earlier meditations first. By being able to hold your body, and your breath in meditative awareness for long periods of time, you will be much better placed to skillfully accept the emotions that come up for you. For this reason as well, do take the advice to start gently and choose people you have gentle disagreements with first, until your confidence improves.

This meditation can be very powerful. I remember being on a retreat only a year after I had felt so low and been carried off to hospital in the police van, and I was getting deeper and deeper into the loving kindness meditation. Suddenly I started to feel the most intense pleasure running through my body. The more I tried not to be distracted by it, the more intense the pleasure came. It was as if soft loving bubbles of intense pleasure energy was dripping in waves through me in a rapturous harmonious dance. So intense was the pleasure I experienced throughout my whole body I could barely stand it. It was the most intense sensation of pleasure I have ever had. I may never have such pleasure again in meditation, who knows. But I will never forget it. And it was all the more remarkable given I had been in a place of such pain not so long before. I cannot promise you will experience such pleasure in meditation yourself. If it can happen for me though, it may also surely happen for you too.

Variations on the Loving Kindness Meditation.

Once you have become skilled at using the loving kindness meditation with relatively safe people, you can start introducing people you have a lot of difficulty with. These can be either people in your life right now, or people you have had historic problems with, even people who have died.

Another variation of the loving kindness meditation is to do the whole thing on oneself. If you remember I discussed how very often we could be conflicted in our relationship with ourselves. Part of us wants to do one thing, other parts of us want to go in different directions. Well we can bring each part of us into the meditation. The part of our personality we like. The part of us that is our sensible head or a good friend to us. A part of that is that we don't know very well. Finally, for the difficult person, choose a part of us that we have trouble accepting. It is worth spending a little time being clear before you meditate what parts of you to bring into the meditation.

If you remember, I started by saying loving kindness was one of the four 'heavenly abodes, the other ones being compassion, sympathetic joy and equanimity. Another variation of this meditation is to develop one of the other 'heavenly abodes'.

I would also add a fifth 'heavenly abode' to the list: Gratitude. Our life may not be quite what we want right now, but I imagine there is a lot you can be grateful for. At the very least you have been taught how to read, so you can at least read this book and learn what you need to do to achieve peace from your stress, anxiety and depression!

Indeed, research suggests that spending some time every day being grateful for what you have got in your life, rather than spending time on what you haven't got, is essential to being happy and content with life.[9] Using the structure of this meditation to be grateful to yourself and the other people in your life, including the people you have difficulty with, is a sure way to build your capacity for joy.

Yesterday I touched a moment of deep pain. This inevitably happens when we meditate, especially if we take time, like I have done, to escape from the pressures of routine ... to just become more aware.

I was taking a mindful walk on the beach. Memories of my loving friend, Norma, came to mind. I became very grateful for a gift of money she made me before her death. That gift paid for the computer on which I write, and bought the space and time I needed to write this book. Her generosity has now reached you.

As I became aware of my loss, I became aware of what Norma meant

---

[9] e.g. see McCullough, M. E., Tsang, J., & Emmons, R. A. (2004). Gratitude in intermediate affective terrain: Links of grateful moods to individual differences and daily emotional experience. Journal of Personality and Social Psychology, 86, 295-309. Or Emmons, R. A., & McCullough, M. E. (2003). Counting blessings versus burdens: An experimental investigation of gratitude and subjective well-being in daily life. Journal of Personality and Social Psychology, 84, 377-389

to me, and how very grateful to her I was for so many things. She was one of the handful of people who still believed in me when things were bad, even when I had lost all hope for myself.

As I walked on the beach, I felt a pain welling up in my chest, around the solar plexus. I gave the pain space, hoping it would go away, but it grew stronger. Strange isn't it how we hold our pain in our bodies? How I had been holding this pain in my body all this time. The intensity soon subsided, but it has remained. Or at least, I have been aware of it all day. Just being there. Not letting me forget what it means.

I have come to an impasse. Part of me wishes to run, to escape, in music, in alcohol, in the company of others. I choose another option. To surrender to what is. Fully, completely. To help me, I will use all the resources I am teaching you in this book. Nothing more, nothing less. To do so will require courage, and I feel the temptation to pull back. But I won't.

I meditated on the discomfort in my chest using a mixture of loving kindness and the 'enlightenment technique' I will teach you in Chapter 9. I was then mindful of the sensation for some time afterword.

The sensation of pain in my solar plexus didn't go away, if anything there was a slight heightening of the sensations, and an awareness that this, in fact, is a subtle holding of numerous pains.

Of course these are subtle sensing's. Long gone are the crude stresses and irritations of the first few days. Of 'text-gate'. These are delicate, deeply held pains. In my awareness of the pain, in the writing in the here and now, I have a profound sense of calm, and the hint, for the first time in a while, of a comfortable wellbeing.

As I stay with the sensations and feelings in my chest, it comes to my awareness that it is a deep wound. A wound of separation. Not just the wound of separation from Norma in her passing, but the wound of separation from my surrogate family at 18, and the wound of separation from my birth family, and my mother in particular, in a dramatic incident at the age of 7. It is the wound of a child's catastrophic loss of innocence.

I look deeper. This time trying not to label. Trying not to categorize.

I hug myself for comfort as if I were 7. I give the little boy the love, acceptance and information he needed.

Then it dawns on me, who would I be without this pain. It is my story, it is me. I go deeper.

I become aware of the rejection that is wrapped up within the sensations and pain.

There is awareness that oral addictions pacify and comfort this pain.

Intellectually I know I don't have to keep re-experiencing this hurt, retelling this story, but it doesn't help. I try and focus mindfully some more.

I bring the healing power of loving kindness to the pain of my 7 year old self.

"I forgive myself"
"I forgive myself"
"I forgive myself"

"It's the adults who are letting you down"

"I forgive myself."

I continue to pay attention and the pain persists. But the ego is subtle. I realize I'm paying attention in order that the pain should go. So even subtly, I'm still resisting the pain, rather than surrendering completely.

After two hours of meditation and mindfulness of feelings, I feel calm, and my extremities feel incredibly relaxed, peaceful, alive and, above all, comfortable. But the pain and sensations in my solar plexus persist. Looks like there will be more to say on this one.

I tried to get to sleep. My ego shouted back louder than ever. I tossed and turned for hours having future arguments with people. The theme was people not meeting my needs. My ego, not getting what it wants.

I awoke in the morning late feeling wretched. I knew I had to look after myself. My ego, kicking at my heels, still ruminating over the future arguments from the night before. I try to be mindful and bring myself back to the now. Reminding myself I'm in no danger. But the seductive pleasure of the rumination is too compelling.

I discover an immovable 'I' at the center of my being. An 'I' that would rather die than compromise. Unyielding. I dig deeper, maybe it, the 'I', the indignant 'I', is a hurt and wounded seven year old created for stability in a world that was disintegrating. A world that was failing to meet my needs.

It makes sense now. This is the 'I' I wanted to kill in the past when I said I wanted to kill myself. It is this immovable 'I' I want to destroy. I resolve to bring kindly awareness to the immovable I.

When I observe the 'I', it speaks from the pain in the solar plexus, as if the pain gives it its energy, gives it its voice.

This is the 'I" that becomes outraged when it is not seen, acknowledged, and yielded to. This is the unlovely 'I', that when it speaks, others feel fear and become wary. This is the 'I' that fought and kept me alive, when the world became insane. This is the unmovable core of a very frightened seven year old child. This is the 'I' I took out to play in my 20s because he had no childhood of his own.

This is the 'I' I no longer need as a back stop safety position, but don't know how to live without. I would be softer, kinder maybe, and that would be good, but I may be vulnerable without the 'I' to protect me.

I imagine been squashed paper thin by a steam roller, then just popping back into full three dimensional shape after the threat has passed. Is this what it could be like? Yielding. A different kind of resilience. A resilience that knows nothing in the world can actually touch, change or destroy me. Not even death.

I become aware of the pain and sensations in my solar plexus. I see and hear the screams the child wanted to make, should have been able to make, but was silenced.

Young Me:
"Let me go. Let me go."
Older Me:
"I'm your older self, I've come back through time to help you. To heal you. To love you."

"Yes lash out. Hurt me if you want."

"Kick. Scream. I'm here for you."

"I know you don't really want to hurt me, you just want to make contact."

"I feel your kicks and punches. I hear your screams. I feel your pain with you."

In the irrationality of the instinct dominated maelstrom of my seven year old child, ego was violently, and prematurely, brought into being. A hard, violently angry and repressed ego, that keeps me safe from further abuse and lives in my chest, in my solar plexus. I learned to sooth it with cigarettes. Bathing it in warm smoke.

The young me sobs unyieldingly.

He's pacified now. Sleepy.

Not gone, but starting to dissolve into non being.

He sucks his thumb, and regresses, ... gently returning to source.

Then, dramatically, the very core of evil, a crazed insanity, snarls back in one last gasp for life, for continuity. I bring loving kindness to this part of 'I', of me, too. I have no need of you anymore. You too can also return to source. Just consciousness returning home. I love you.

8.

Mindfulness.

I love skiing. Ever since I was a child, I have tried to go on at least one skiing trip a year. There is nothing more exhilarating for me than setting off down a mountain and feeling my body in flow with gravity and the elements. Sometimes, as I look out over my balcony here in Tunisia, I see groups of people racing water scooters up and down the coast. I imagine they feel something similar to when I go skiing, the past and future disappearing, and caught up in the thrill of the moment.

Dangerous sports, it seems to me, all have this one thing in common. It is in the nature of the activity that it compels you to live completely and utterly in the moment. If I lose the here and now when skiing, I simply fall flat on my face. I can't ski and ruminate!

Meditation, as you have been learning, is a practice that brings you back to the present moment repeatedly. It is surely less risky than dangerous sports, but with practice, no less effective.

A common mistake with people who learn to meditate is they think it is an end in itself. You learn to meditate, so to speak, so you can meditate. This, however, could be no further from the truth. The point of meditating, of practicing and being in the moment, is so *you can live more fully in the moment.* If you meditate every day, and then make no effort to live your daily life more fully present, then you have surely missed the point.

When people talk of living mindfully, or living with awareness, this is what they are referring to. Using the skills practiced in meditation to live more fully in the present, or mindfully, right now. You can do anything with full attention, except possibly sleep (although some yogis claim even this is possible). One way of understanding enlightenment is it is a person who has perfected living completely in the moment. The corollary of this is that whenever you live fully, completely, in the moment, then you awaken to enlightenment. Even if it's just for a few seconds.

Why is this important for someone who suffers from stress, anxiety and depression? Well, if you think about it, people who are stressed, anxious or depressed, are caught up in things that have happened, the past, or might happen, the future. You might say, "but I'm scared of spiders, and that's happening right now, I can see the spider in front of me". Well at the moment you are scared, this is true, but you are scared of what might happen, that the spider might bite you, and you will die, for example. So really you are scared because you are caught up In the future. In fact rumination, which is a central concept for stress, anxiety and depression sufferers, as you now know, is all about the past or the future. You can't ruminate about the present, it is simply not possible.

You might say "Well what about emergency situations, surely people are scared then?" Well not really, if there is a genuine life or death situation happening right now, you are completely focussed, completely present, and you do whatever you need to do to save life and limb. When the emergency is over, you might become scared of what could have happened, or even upset about what did happen, or you should have done. But at the time of the emergency, the past and the future disappear, so there is no space for stress, anxiety or depression. This is what the reactive mind was designed to do. It is only when we turn our reactive mind to the past or the future that we get problems.

I remember once sitting in one of those pool bars with my buddies in a tropical beach resort in India. I was up to my waist in water sipping my gin and tonic, chatting to the other people around the bar. Suddenly to my left, a young toddler jumped into the water which was quite deep, but she couldn't swim and started to drown. She sank like a stone in front of my eyes. Instantly, her father jumped in after her. Unfortunately he couldn't swim either, and he was out of his depth, so he started to drown as well. Suddenly we all swung into action, and I have no recollection of how, but we got father and daughter out of the water, and administered the kiss of life. It was only after the pair was dispatched in an emergency ambulance and we all re-gathered around the bar, that we started actually to feel the enormity of what had just happened. We were all pretty shaken, but at the time we had no time for 'what ifs', we just did what we needed to do to save life.

So here's the deal: the more fully you are able to live in the present, the more past and future seems to disappear, the less stress, anxiety and depression you will experience.

Of course you may not necessarily feel wonderful all the time, but however you feel, if you are fully present to the here and now, you will be able to access the same peace and calm and loving attention you can now generate in meditation. It will be there for you in your daily life. Of course it is not easy, that's why you need to practice.

So now you have started to build your meditation skills, it is time to start bringing those skills for present moment living into your daily life. To get you started, I suggest the following five practices.

1. **Mindful eating.**

We literally are what we eat; yet we often pay little attention to what or how we eat. Often these days eating has become something we multitask, say while watching the TV, so our awareness of it is even more diminished.

I will describe eating a single nut mindfully. As the other mindfulness practices invite a similar narrative, I will only describe this one in detail. Obviously if you are allergic to nuts try something you can eat, like a grape instead!

First, make sure you have 15 minutes or so without distraction.

Place a single nut on a plate, and take some time to notice it fully. I know what I'm like when I eat nuts, usually a handful go into the mouth straight from the packet, and I never even get chance to look, never mind appreciate the nuts I eat.

Take several minutes to look deeply into the colors, textures and shape of the nut.

What feelings or sensations does the nut evoke in you?

Does the nut evoke any memories for you?

As with meditation, you may find your mind wanders, that's OK. Just bring your mind back to the nut and carry on.

Once you have visually examined the nut in some detail, you might then try to invoke your other senses. What does the nut feel like and smell like?
Again, check in with yourself and notice what thoughts, feelings and memories the nut evokes for you.

You might then 'interrogate' the nut more deeply.

How did it get to be on your plate? You don't necessarily need to know in detail, so it's ok to imagine.

Notice you can move back in the supply chain all the way back to the time the nut was being grown.

At each point in the supply chain, large numbers of unnamed and unknown individuals helped in the growing, picking, transportation, labeling, distribution and sale of that nut.

You might reflect what feelings your have for these people, without whom the nut would not be available for you to eat.

Thinking deeply about the nut in this way, you may come to appreciate how deeply interconnected we are with people we have never met.

What kind of lives do these people have?

Do they want to be happy and love and be loved, just like us?

Ponder these, and any other questions you have before 'interrogating' the nut further.

You may wish to consider what conditions were required in order for the nut to grow. What sunshine conditions, nutritional conditions and water conditions were needed?

Taking just the water for now, you might reflect on where the water came from, that each molecule of water will have had its own history of being in the sea, in rivers, in clouds and in mist and rain. Furthermore this history may have gone on for thousands, if not hundreds of thousands of years, before the particular water molecules in the nut arrive on your plate.

You might choose to reflect that this nut reflects not only a human interconnection, but also a material interconnection, possibly tying you, the nut and this moment to the whole planet, and perhaps the whole universe.

Looked at this way, this moment is perfect, just as it is.

You might also reflect on the other aspects of the content of the nut, like the minerals it is made of, or the sunshine it 'contains', and how they connect you to the universe in this moment.

When you are through with that, it's finally time to start to eat your nut.
Place the nut in your mouth, but do not chew or move it about. What do you notice?

What changes occur in your body?

What conditions are necessary to allow your body to respond in the way that it just did?

What feelings, emotions, sensations and memories occur as you experience the nut in your mouth?

When you are ready, roll the nut around your mouth. Notice the sensations, feelings, and textures, etc., which emerge from playing with the nut in this way.

Now, finally, allow the nut to be crushed by your teeth, and chew very slowly.

What happens to your mouth, how does finally eating the nut make you feel?

Continue 'interrogating' your experience of eating the nut until no further traces of it can be found in your mouth.

This, then, gives you a good feel about what is meant by doing something mindfully. Yes we do something slowly. Yes we also do something with greater care. But we are also doing it fully in the moment, and giving ourselves permission to experience the activity fully, and possibly in new and novel ways.

There are thousand of other lines of enquiry you could have taken. You could eat a nut mindfully every day for the rest of your life and never have the same experience twice.

After you have tried eating a nut mindfully, you might try gradually increasing the size and complexity of the food you eat until you can eat a full meal mindfully.

2. **Mindful walking.**

There is a long tradition of mindful walking in the east. For westerners it is less common, so it is probably wise to choose where you walk carefully. A garden or a park would probably facilitate a careful slow walk rather than on the way to catch a bus on a busy street.

Mindful walking requires the same care as eating a nut mindfully. You may choose to walk more slowly, at least at first. Notice all the sensations that occur throughout your whole body as you transfer weight from one foot to the next.

My experience of this practice is it also changes the way I experience the world around me. I start noticing things in the environment that I hadn't been aware of before. It's up to you if you allow yourself to be drawn into the world, or you stay tuned in to your body. Whatever choice you make, however, do it with complete awareness.

Start small, say with just five minutes, and then increase gradually for as far as you want to go.

If ever you feel it might be appropriate to teach mindfulness to a child, consider starting with mindful walking: for some reason they seem to love it.

3. **Mindful self-care.**

Self-care makes for a great mindfulness practice, not least because we have to perform these tasks all the time, and we normally do them automatically, without really thinking. This is great practice because our habit energy will automatically take us in a particular direction, and you can mindfully decide whether you do or do not want to go with that.

Self-care also gives us the opportunity to express loving kindness towards our bodies. Our habitual self-care routines may miss out certain parts of our body, and focus on others. We can be curious about this. We might also notice things that may need attention, say by a health care provider. It is amazing what we can miss simply because we do not pay attention.

While on this writing retreat I have done mindful face washes, shaves and showers. For some reason, I seem to have 'interrogated' the contents of the products I am using. Are they animal, vegetable or mineral? This had never occurred to me before, but obviously has animal welfare implications. I also then got into a bit of emotional guilt for having never considered this deeply before, but that simply gave me something else to pay attention to, and be curious about.

4. **Mindful emotion space.**

Becoming more mindful of our emotions is really important if we feel stressed, anxious or depressed. The reason for this is we often tell ourselves a story about our emotion that is not actually true. I often encourage clients to record and notice their problem feelings and behaviors throughout the day. Often they discover, to their surprise, that they are not as stressed, anxious or depressed as they have been telling themselves they are. This can then encourage them to see that some of the things they do, some of the time, actually help them.

Start by allocating three slots of two minutes during the day. You clearly need to choose times that will facilitate quiet reflection. Many clients then set up regular alarms so they don't forget.

When it's time for your mindful emotion space, take the time to notice what you are feeling, and any sensations you may be experiencing as well. Often our initial 'gloss' of, say, 'anxious', hides a more subtle or nuanced feeling state. Often even though our overall feeling tone may be negative, there may be positive feeling tone around for you as well. Take the time to notice both.

It is important to just let the feelings, sensations and emotions be there. With this mindfulness practice we are not trying to understand or make sense of the experience, just bring a kindly, caring and non-judgmental awareness to the experience. Sometimes, as happened with me yesterday, the feelings can intensify by paying attention. Notice your reaction to this, again non-judgmentally, and stay with it. More often, the feeling tone changes, simply by paying attention, and can sometimes even fade completely. Whether your feelings intensify or fade, just observe what happens without judgment.

Once you have become used to three sessions of two minutes a day, you can gradually start to increase the frequency and length of sessions.

5. **Mindful appreciation.**

In life, we always have a choice. We can focus on the problems, or we can focus on the solutions. We can focus on what's broken, or we can focus on what's working. We can focus on the bad, or we can focus on the good. I know why my stressed, anxious or depressed clients focus on the bad stuff. It's the same reason I did. We believe that if we focus on the bad stuff, we can sort it out, and then after that, we can get the good stuff.

There is an alternative: focus on what's working, what's enjoyable and what's fulfilling in your life already. If we could focus a little more on that, actually the bad stuff tends to just take care of itself.

So, if you're stressed, instead of paying attention to all the things you haven't done, pay attention to all the things you have done. If you're anxious, instead of paying attention to the things in your life that scare you, pay attention to the things that bring you safety and security. If you're depressed, instead of paying attention to the things about yourself, your future and the world that you don't like, pay attention to the things you do like.

Of course if you are profoundly stressed, anxious or depressed right now, it may be a struggle finding those things. We may also be in a lifetime pattern of refusing to see them. But the good is out there, if you take the time to look. The better and more skilled you become at paying attention to the good in your life, the happier you will feel.

In this practice, then, choose something about you or your life that you do appreciate. Even if it's very small. Even if it's as Anthony Robins, the Life Coach and motivational speaker says, 'thank God my feet don't stink today'! Find something you can appreciate, and take the time to really see it. 'Interrogate' it as surely as if it were the nut I described earlier. If you take the time to really see what you appreciate, you will not only learn something about that, but you might learn something about yourself too.

As with all these practices, start small and build up. Five minutes on something small is great to start. As you develop the practice you can either spend more time with one item, or spend the same amount of time with more items.

This practice, more than any other, has the potential to emancipate you from the turmoil of despair. Eventually you come to learn something very simple, but very profound. Actually the world is perfect, just the way it is.

9.

The Enlightenment Meditation – or 'Just Sitting'.

It's mid morning. I managed to get to the hotel breakfast. At about 10 am, a torrent of a dozen or so texts arrived. It was a week now since I go so upset about my friend 'ignoring me'. For some reason I now have been sent all of her texts a week late. Here was the concrete proof she had not been ignoring me. Unfortunately she seemed to have been getting increasingly upset and concerned by my escalating accusations of suggesting she was doing just that! Seeing the distress in her texts, I felt guilty and immediately sent her an update, and even more apologies.

It's a beautiful but rugged day in Tunisia. The wind is blowing ferociously. The sea is rough, and as I sit in the hotel garden and watch the waves crashing, two sparrows land some way in front of me. One, then the other, jumps up into the gusting wind, gets carried backwards, and then lands. They repeat this jest over and over. Yet when they choose to fly away, the wind appears to offer no resistance. They are gone.

Tourists are encamping themselves on the beach. They have come for a beach holiday, and they are determined to have one, whatever else the sea and the wind have in mind.

As I return to my room, I find myself in an old, but familiar head narrative. I catch myself. This is nothing other than the pain I penetrated so deeply the other day. I ask myself, "Am I damaged right now?" Of course the answer is no. I smile. My crazy mind was at it again.

In this chapter I'm going to teach you what is a deceptively simple meditation. I call it 'the enlightenment meditation' because, in a way, you are creating the conditions for enlightenment itself. While doing this meditation, you are practicing being enlightened. And in a way, you are.

Like all the mindfulness and meditation techniques that I have been teaching you, the enlightenment meditation has a long history. In the east, a variation of this meditation is practiced in the Zen tradition, and is called Zazen. Traditionally you sit facing a wall for Zazen, the Zen master, who wanders around, hits you from time to time to ensure you are remembering to pay attention!

A gentler version was taught by the Buddhist monk, and founder of the Triratna Buddhist community, Sangahratchita. Here, it is called, 'just sitting', and is an apt description.

In the version I will teach you, it has been crafted to be of particular help for people experiencing stress, anxiety and depression. I will first describe the practice, and then explain how it helps. By now you probably will be able to guess anyway.

The Enlightenment Meditation.

You can do this meditation in one of two ways. You can listen to a recording by downloading one from the selection at philtyson.com/downloads. I have a range to choose from including some with music and binaural beats.

You don't need a recording of course; you can just as effectively follow the instructions below.

Find yourself comfortably in your meditation posture, and ensure you have no interruptions for about 20 minutes.

First, become aware of you body by doing a gentle body scan.

When you can hold your entire body in your awareness, including feelings and sensations, expand your awareness more broadly to include any noises or sounds you can hear in your environment. Listen also, for the silence between the sounds.

When you are able to hold your body, its feelings and sensations, and your environment, in terms of sounds and silences, in awareness (and if you can do this, it is already a great achievement), you are ready to move on to the next stage.

Adopt an attitude of waiting for your mind to start wandering.

As you know already, our minds continually scurry in to disrupt our meditative concentration. In the enlightenment meditation, I invite you to just sit, and wait for this to happen. In so doing, we become awareness itself. It's as simple as that. But of course it is easier to describe than actually do!

In this meditation we have, if you like, set a trap for our habitual thinking mind to fall into. As night follows day, our minds will start their thinking and imagining magic. But we are ready for it. When our minds click into action, just allow the thoughts and images to be there without judgment. Gently return your awareness to the body, the environment, and then again to the waiting. To the anticipation.

It is inevitable that the mind will try to intrude. So it is really important to treat the contents of the mind with kindness when it does occur. No judgment should be made. There is no reason to feel good or bad whatever happens. 'Success' in this meditation, is simply in the having a go. As you cannot help but get caught up in the machinations of your thinking mind, there is absolutely no point in greeting its behavior with anger or disappointment.

As you may have guessed, this meditation is perfect for people who have stress, anxiety or depression. If you have been following my reasoning so far, most of what we get stressed, anxious or depressed about are things that have happened in the past, or that may happen in the future. They are, in other words, creatures of the mind, and the mind alone. In this meditation, we deliberately look for the very start of that process. The thinking process that takes us away from the here and now, and into the past and the future.

It is perhaps the easiest meditation to describe, but possibly the hardest to do. You will be giving yourself a good chance if you spend some time mastering the other mindfulness and meditation techniques I have described earlier. In The Enlightenment Plan, I introduce this meditation after two months of practice of mindfulness and meditation. I think this is about right, but please feel free to follow your own rhythms. For some of you, tackling this meditation may require longer than two months of practice of the other techniques. As with all meditation practices, accept what is, and be kind to yourself.

I was practicing this meditation on a retreat once. It was only 18 months after my experience with the police and the hospital. I had built a solid daily meditation practice at home, and this was now my fourth retreat. I was at the height of my meditative powers.

I was in the flow of doing the enlightenment meditating for half an hour, then being gentle with myself in mindfulness for a further half an hour, and then repeating for the full day. Of course I had breaks for sleep and eating, but I had maintained this routine for several days.

I remember standing outside in one of my breaks. It was a balmy summer evening in the Welsh countryside, and the sun was starting its decline over the hills. I guess it must have been about 7 pm. I was still. Perfectly still. I looked down at my foot. To my amazement, a field mouse was sitting on my right shoe. It was mindlessly cleaning itself, apparently oblivious to me. I was amazed and transfixed, and watched this little creature and its antics until it decided to move on, which was only after several minutes. This was the most incredible experience I have ever had. I was amazed that a creature as wild and as timid as a field mouse could have been so oblivious of me. I imagine I will never have a similar experience again. However, it transformed my understanding of what is possible.

Ultimately both CBT and meditation and mindfulness have the same aim: to identify with the place of observation, including the observer of the mind itself. Through practice, we come to realize we are not our minds. It is more that our minds happen to us. Furthermore, with practice, we can come to longer identify with the mind; however loud it roars, we always have a choice: that choice is to pay attention to something else instead.

In this final meditation, by 'just sitting', we come to taste enlightenment itself. We gently realize we are simply awareness. Everything else, including our stresses, our anxieties, and our depressions, are simply illusion. In the awareness, we find freedom.

10.

Going Deeper.

As we come to the end of our journey together, I hope you are looking forward to starting The Enlightenment Plan (if you haven't already). Each week is described in detail in the Appendix. Just focus on one week at a time and try not to read ahead.

There is a wealth of resources available to help you with the program including downloadable forms, video tutorials, and mp3 guided meditations. Everything you need to complete this program is contained in this book or is available for download from philtyson.com/downloads.

If you find you are struggling, or just want extra support from me and the other students who are following this program, check out my multimedia course, which accompanies this book, at EnlightenmentPlanAcademy.com.

The Enlightenment Plan distills everything I needed to learn and do to beat stress, anxiety and depression. It is my sincere wish that it will do the same for you. You need to know that the surest way to success with this plan is complete immersion and commitment to it. The ten weeks I have outlined in the Appendix are just the start. So how should you deepen your practice? Well there are several things you can do.

1. **Practice more often.**

The aim of The Enlightenment Plan is to give you all the skills and techniques you need to beat stress, anxiety and depression. It is your responsibility to take these practices, and creatively apply them to your unique situation. Pay attention to what works for you, and what doesn't work for you, and follow your own rhythms.

The more you practice the Thinking Form, the meditations, and the mindfulness practices, the quicker will be your complete recovery. I guess it will need an act of faith to get you going, and then pretty quickly, as you start to reap the benefits, faith will be transformed into evidence of your own success, which will continue to propel you forward. This is one of the reasons I encourage you to fill out the Tyson Emotional Distress Scale regularly.

Remember, I started practicing when I had lost everything. I had few friends left, I was depressed, bankrupt, and in poverty. I believed I had no future.

In fact the worse your current situation, the better it might be for you. Sometimes the hardest clients I have to work with are mildly stressed, anxious and depressed. Things are bad for them, but they are not sufficiently motivated by their pain to contemplate the radical transformation they need to feel better. If this is you, then don't wait for things to get worse. Start practicing now, maybe just a little commitment and openness to new ways of thinking now will be all you will need to get your life back on track.

If you are at the end, and feel life has no meaning and the pain is too great to bear. Congratulations! The conditions are right for you to completely and radically let go of the past, and live fully, completely and unwaveringly in the present. You are closer to not only solving your problems, but awakening into complete spiritual enlightenment, than ever you thought possible.

2. **Practice with Other People.**

There is nothing more motivating, in my experience, than embarking on a journey with other people. They are there to share your successes, and to help motivate you when you are struggling.

Most towns and cities these days have meditation and mindfulness classes you can attend. Take the time to find new people that can help you in the next part of your life's journey. They are out there, and what is more, they need help and support too. Help from someone like you.

Remember you can get online support at EnlightenmentPlanAcademy.com.

3. **Go on Retreat.**

You may have noticed during this book that, I often talk about having been on retreat. In fact, I'm writing this book on a meditation, mindfulness and meditation retreat. Indeed, some of my most profound meditative experiences, things that have really changed my life, have happened on retreat.

Retreats are great for deepening your practice. I would suggest planning your first retreat to coincide with the end of The Enlightenment Plan. Having a weekend away to look forward to might just give you something to work towards.

As with everything in meditation and mindfulness, it is important with retreats to be kind to yourself. Start with a weekend beginner's retreat. Once you know what to expect, go for something lasting a week or so.

Unfortunately most retreat centers are from within a faith tradition. However, most retreat centers do not expect you to follow the faith. Respectfully simply do not participate in any rituals that are offered on the retreat for followers of the faith.

Unfortunately, some retreat centers can be pretty basic. I remember the first retreat center I visited thinking it was the nearest thing to camping I had experienced while still being indoors! Many retreat centers only have shared single sex dormitories. Not all retreat centers are so basic, so it is worth shopping around and doing your research. I have stayed in some retreat centers where I have been able to have my own room, and it was up to the standard of a basic good hotel.

If you are attached to your comforts, there is also nothing wrong with doing what I have done in Tunisia. Booking a decent hotel, and cutting yourself off from the world. As you noticed with me, retreats do bring up some deep psychological material, and small things can get way out of proportion. Be prepared for the ride of your life. You may choose to organize some support at home if you find things tough going.

I'm often asked if I offer retreats myself. The answer to this is not at the moment, but I may well start doing in the future. Follow me at my blogs to get the latest information.

4. **Stay consistent.**

To get the most out of mindfulness and meditation, it is best to stay consistent. Meditating once a week for a year will probably do you more good than once a day for fifty-two days. It is important to be realistic with yourself. If you do fall out of your routine, try not to be discouraged and too hard on yourself. It happens to all of us, especially at the beginning. Just gently, and patiently, start practicing again, building it up slowly.

So I guess this is the end. I still have some writing to do on The Enlightenment Plan, so my retreat, meditation, mindfulness and writing will continue for a few more days. But this is the last time I will be checking in with you. I feel like I have been here both a long time, and yet merely an instant. I can't quite believe it has come to an end.

As I write, the wind is working itself up to frenzy outside my balcony. It feels like the finale of a long piece of music. I'm thinking of you, the reader. Thank you for reading this book. I hope you use this opportunity to radically transform your life. If you do, I would love to hear about it. If you decide the time is not right for total immersion, then I hope you have got something from reading the book, and who knows, it may have sown a few seeds which will sprout in the years to come.

I hope you have enjoyed reading this book. If you have, and even if you haven't, you can help spread the word and give me some feedback by leaving a quick review now on your Amazon or similar account. Your feedback will make a difference and help others to access this valuable information.

With Gratitude and Thanks.

Phil Tyson Ph.D.

Tunisia, 2013.

Further Reading

If you are interested in cognitive behavioral therapy and how it might help you with stress, anxiety and depression, I can recommend the following two books:

- **Mind Over Mood: Change How You Feel By Changing the Way You Think** by Denis Greenberger and Christine Padesky. Guilford Press.

This book's basic message is to look for the evidence that the world is how you think it is. It also contains loads of useful information and helpful worksheets to help you beat your problems.

- **Feeling Good Handbook** by David D. Burns. Penguin.

This book is great if you are interested in the unhelpful ways our mind creates our perception of reality. It also contains loads of useful information and helpful work sheets.

If you are interested in mindfulness, I can recommend the following:

- **Miracle of Mindfulness** by Thich Nhat Hanh. Rider.

This book was written by a Zen Buddhist monk and peace activist about the time of the Vietnam War when his people were under attack. A remarkable and inspiring work that will stand the test of time.

- **The Power of Now** by Eckhart Tolle. Hodder paperbacks.

This is a more recently written book that has already become a legend. You will be inspired to leave your problems behind by living in the now. It can get a bit metaphysical from time to time, but it is an inspirational read.

If you are interested in the metta bhavana meditation, try the following:

- **Loving Kindness: The Revolutionary Art of Happiness** by Haron Salzberg. Shambhala Publications Inc.

Finally, if you still need convincing all this has a scientific background, try the following:

- **Buddha's Brain: The Practical Neuroscience of Happiness, Love and Wisdom.** by Rick Hanson and Richard Mendius. New Harbinger Publications.

You can also find me at my blogs:

ScienceofEnlightenment.com

And

MenandMentalHealth.com

And

TheRenouncer.com

Appendix - The Enlightenment Plan

So you now have all the information you need to start The Enlightenment Plan. It is a ten week course designed to radically shift your consciousness from one caught up in stress, anxiety and depression, to one focused in the here and now with a creative, compassionate and calm mind. The aim is to do this in two ways.

1. Using core cognitive behavioral techniques for identifying and challenging your habitual mind's reactive thinking habits, and
2. Using ancient mindfulness and meditation techniques to awaken a more peaceful and creative frame of mind.

This program uniquely combines these techniques to produce a powerful engine for change.

You can monitor your progress on The Enlightenment Plan, with The Enlightenment Plan Progress Chart, which can be downloaded from philtyson.com/downloads where you will also find all the other resources you will need including the Tyson Emotional Distress Scale (TEDS) and The Thinking Form.

I have given you all the instructions you need to perform the meditations accurately earlier within the text, so if you prefer, simply refer to them. Some people, however, like guided meditations with or without sound to help them. If you want to experiment with music and binaural beats, or indeed have all the meditations available at different lengths, you will need to download these separately. These albums can be purchased directly at a discount from my website at philtyson.com/downloads or from your online music store.

This program is life changing, however you have to participate wholeheartedly in order to get the benefits. The more you practice the techniques, the quicker you will make progress. The suggestions given in this plan are the minimum you need for success. If you are ambivalent about proceeding, now is probably the time to stop. You will only give yourself a failure experience. Better to wait for a moment when you are more receptive. This book, and the downloads, will be waiting for you when you return.

If you want more support, check out the multimedia online course that accompanies this book with video tutorials, all the materials and CD's included to download, weekly encouragement and a forum where you can hang out with me and the other students. Check it out at EnlightenmentPlanAcademy.com now …

The Plan.

At the beginning of each week, you will be asked to complete the Tyson Emotional Distress Scale (TEDS). This will give you a good measure of your current levels of stress, anxiety and depression, so you can chart your progress.

I suggest only reading one week's instructions at a time. There is little to be gained from pre-reading ahead of where you actually are. In fact some of the instructions and teachings will just confuse you.

So collect all the resources you need, and we can begin. You will need:

1. The Enlightenment Plan Progress Chart.
2. The Tyson Emotional Distress Scale.
3. The Thinking form.
4. Any CDs you feel you may need.

All are described in detail and available for purchase at <u>philtyson.com/downloads</u>. Check it out now.

Week 1.

Complete your first TEDS self-assessment measure. Bear in mind how you have been feeling over the last week. Don't over analyze the questions. It is best to go with your gut reaction. Record your TEDS score in The Enlightenment Plan Progress Chart.

It is worth mentioning that the TEDS does give you a good measure of your symptoms right now, but from week to week it will vary. It is rare for people to experience a gentle steady decline in their symptoms, although this is possible. It is normal for the symptoms to vary from week to week. Try not to be too demoralized if your score goes up some weeks, this is perfectly normal. What is important is collecting the evidence so you can review your progress after 10 weeks.

The aims of the first week are very modest. They are:

1. To start recording your negative reactive thinking on The Thinking Form, and
2. To experiment meditating with the Stress Buster meditation for 5 minutes, on 5 separate days.

Most people can find 5 minutes to meditate, but different people have different pressures on their time. Try experimenting with the time of day you meditate. It suits some people to meditate in the morning, and some in the evening. Both are acceptable, and neither is better than the other.

Start also to record your negative thoughts by writing them in The Thinking Form. Don't worry about challenging these thoughts just yet, that will come next week. In a way, becoming aware of your thinking is a mindfulness practice in its own right. Try to write the thoughts down in real time if possible. Try also to write the thoughts down in as much detail as possible. Don't worry if you find this difficult. As you become more aware of the workings of your mind, you will get much better as The Enlightenment Plan proceeds.

Overcoming Common Obstacles.

The two most common obstacles are:
1. Not being able to find the time to practice, and
2. Not being able to find the space to practice.
I will discuss each in turn.

First, not having the time. Now the simple fact is that anybody can find five minutes to practice a simple technique, so if you are convinced you have not got the time, here are a few questions you can ask yourself.

1. What do I currently do that takes five minutes that I could stop doing for a while?
2. List all the reasons finding five minutes to start this program would be a good thing to do. Also list why finding five minutes would be a bad thing to do.
3. Look for all the evidence that telling yourself you don't have time for things is a good thing to believe. Look for all the evidence that telling yourself you don't have the time for good things is a bad thing.
4. Make a list of all the reasons learning to meditate would be a good skill to have and practice.

5. If there were an emergency, would you find five minutes to leave the building or find safety?
6. If answering these questions doesn't help, then this program possibly isn't going to help you. You really do have a problem. I suggest a coma!

Second, not having the space. I often find that this question reveals not so much about not having the space, as not being able to negotiate the space. Often people do have the space to find five minutes on their own to meditate, but the problem is negotiating the time within their household. This may simply mean having a serious chat with your partner to make five minutes available to you. Perhaps he or she could look after the children and take responsibility so the kids don't disturb you. If you do hear them outside the room, or heaven forbid, they do come in, see this as an opportunity to practice the acceptance of what is. Simply accept that they have disturbed you, and do whatever you need to do to reestablish the boundary. Do it calmly. If you do this quietly and often enough they will get the message. It can be helpful to put a 'Meditation in Progress' or 'Do Not Disturb' sign up on the door just in case the partner or the kids forget.

So I hope this serves you. I suggest you get started right now!

After you have completed each meditation, give yourself a little reward, even if it is just a self-congratulatory pat on the back. Don't forget to give yourself a tick in the Progress Form.

You are, of course, welcome to practice more than the five times suggested, but make sure you do manage the five times during the week.

At the end of the week, collect the Thinking Forms together, and try to find any patterns that keep cropping up. You might want to make a note of them.

Once you have completed 5 meditations, well done, you're ready to move on to Week 2.

If for any reason you have not managed 5 meditations, don't worry, sometimes life can get in the way: just start again from the beginning of Week 1.

Week 2.

Congratulations! Starting anything new is always the hardest part, and you have managed to get up and running. Please don't underestimate what a great achievement that is. Well done!

Complete your second TEDS self-assessment measure now. Bear in mind how you have been feeling over the last week. Don't over analyze the questions. It is best to go with your gut reaction. Record your TEDS score in The Enlightenment Plan Progress Chart.

Sometimes people find that focusing their attention on their negative reactive thinking patterns can make them feel worse in the short term. If this has happened to you, try not to worry, this is perfectly normal.

Have you noticed yet how easy it is for your mind to wander in the meditation? I'm sure you have. Just remember to be kind to yourself. The meditations work long term just as well if you are able to focus or if your focusing is bad. What is important is the moment you notice you have lost you concentration. Well done, you just woke up! In fact the more you forget, the more opportunities to 'wake up' there are.

In Week 2 we have two aims:

1. Start completing the full thought record before and after every meditation, and
2. Increase your Stress Buster meditation to 15 minutes for 5 times during the week.

Now you have worked out when is the best time for you to meditate, and you have sorted out all those practical details, we can start to really get going. By doing the Stress Buster meditation for 15 minutes, you will start to notice subtle changes in your daily experience of stress, anxiety and depression. Don't get me wrong, you still have some way to go, but most people say they experience some benefit after just one week of the 15 minute meditations.

Continue to collect your negative thinking habits in real time like you did in Week 1. This time, AFTER you have done your daily meditation, go back to the thoughts in the Thinking Form, and try and identify the kinds of thinking habits you have been using. Also start getting into the habit of looking for the evidence to support, and disconfirm, your view of the world. When you have gone through this in detail using the Thinking Form, try writing down a more balanced or creative way to view your life situations. It doesn't matter if it doesn't feel compelling. What is important is you are starting to offer up alternatives to your mind's automatic thinking. Over time this will change things for you.

The more time you spend on this, the more you will get out of it. Remember this is a two stage process, being mindful of unhelpful ways of thinking about the world, followed by the creative generations of alternatives. Meditating between stage one and stage two helps to get you out of reactive mind and into creative mind.

Again, don't worry too much if you still struggle with this. As you practice you will get better at spotting the patterns and challenging them.

The Stress Buster Meditation is a great meditation for helping to relieve stress; especially if you hold stress in your body, in areas like your shoulders. Now you know how to do this meditation, you can always choose to use it in your everyday life if you feel particularly stressed or anxious.

After you have completed each meditation, give yourself a little reward, even if it is just a self-congratulatory pat on the back. Don't forget to give yourself a tick in The Enlightenment Plan Progress Chart.

You are, of course, welcome to practice more than the five times suggested, but make sure you do manage the five times during the week.

At the end of the week, collect The Thinking Forms together, and try to find any patterns that keep cropping up. You might want to make a note of them.

If for any reason you have not managed 5 meditations, don't worry, sometimes life can get in the way: just start again from the beginning of Week 2. If this is the second consecutive week you haven't been able to stick to the routine, reflect on what has gone wrong, put remedies in place, and start again from Week 1.

If you have completed 5 meditations, well done, you're ready to move onto Week 3.

Week 3.

Complete your third TEDS self-assessment measure. Bear in mind how you have been feeling over the last week. Don't over analyze the questions. It is best to go with your gut reaction. Record your TEDS score in The Enlightenment Plan Progress Chart.

So how was week 2? For most people, learning mindfulness and meditation (and CBT for that matter) is a slow burn. It is sometimes described as like going out for a walk in a mist: eventually, even though it doesn't rain, you get wet. I'd be surprised if you didn't get some initial benefit from the first two weeks, but I would expect it to be small. Keep going, the best is yet to come!

The most common response at about this time is 'I'm not getting what I want', or 'I'm not getting what I expected'.

Remember the joke I retold at the start of Chapter 5, the one about the drowning man. The message of that joke was that sometimes having preconceived ideas of what the solution can look like actually means you turn down the help you need.

Right now you are stressed, anxious or depressed. I would be surprised if you didn't already have a view of what the solution would look like, and what you need to do to achieve it. The conscious reactive mind loves comparisons, and by defining an end point too tightly, it will mean you will never get what you really need, lasting peace from the mind itself.

With mindfulness and meditation, we are not so much focusing on your current difficulties, more creating a space for where your current difficulties are simply irrelevant, as they have been transcended. The 'solution', in other words, may look nothing like what you are expecting. Just be open a little bit more to that possibility and press on for now.

In week 3 we have two aims:

1. Complete the Thought Form before and after every meditation, and
2. Start practicing the first two stages of the mindfulness of breathing meditation, that's 10 minutes, 5 times in the week.

With The Thought Form, this week I'd like you to become a little more curious about your reactive thinking habits. Go a little bit deeper into your thinking processes, the way you create your own despair.

Sometimes when I work with clients, they find The Thought Form really difficult to complete in any detail. All they seem to be able to say is the headline, such as 'feeling sad about Jane leaving me', or 'Upset about rejection at school'. If this is you, it is great that you are becoming more mindful, but I need you to go a little deeper. Here are some questions you can ask to interrogate the experience your mind is generating for you.

"What does it say about me that I have this problem?"
"What is the significance of this for my life?"
"Because I think like this, it shows me that …."

In other words my invitation is to go beyond the headline of your suffering, and into its meaning. This, of course, will be different for every person. The headline problem might be, 'Girlfriend walks out on me', and for one person what this means might be they will now be lonely, for another person this means they might feel humiliated at the rejection, and for another person they might be relieved. We are all different, and what these circumstances mean for you is the important thing

Turning now to the mindfulness of breathing meditation.

This meditation is a little harder than the Stress Buster meditation, in part because you have more space in which your mind can wander. I know I keep saying this, but it is so important, your mind will wander, and there is nothing wrong with that. Just celebrate the moments when you become aware of the mind wandering. You have woken up to the here and the now.

The mindfulness of breathing is also a more powerful meditation. If your mind is scattered and poorly focused, this meditation will help you separate what is important from what is not.

Often people exit the mindfulness of breathing with a clear idea of what they need to do next. My suggestion is if it is in your interests to do so, act on this moment of insight straightaway. You may not be able to do everything, but you can at least start, even if it is just a small thing.

After you have completed each meditation, give yourself a little reward, even if it is just a self-congratulatory pat on the back. Don't forget to give yourself a tick in the Progress Form.

You are, of course, welcome to practice more than the five times suggested, but make sure you do manage the five times during the week.

At the end of the week, collect your Thinking Forms together, and try to find any patterns that keep cropping up. You might want to make a note of them.

If for any reason you have not managed 5 meditations, don't worry, sometimes life can get in the way: just start again from the beginning of Week 3. If this is the second consecutive week you haven't been able to stick to the routine, reflect on what has gone wrong, put remedies in place, and start again from Week 1.

If you have completed 5 meditations, well done, you're ready to move on to Week 4.

Week 4.

Complete your fourth TEDS self-assessment measure. Bear in mind how you have been feeling over the last week. Don't over analyze the questions. It is best to go with your gut reaction. Record your TEDS score in The Enlightenment Plan Progress Chart.

You are making really good progress. You already into week 4!

This week, we have two aims:

1. Complete the Thought Form before and after every meditation, and
2. Start practicing the full mindfulness of breathing meditation, which is 20 minutes, 5 times during the week.

What most people find is that when they start doing the full mindfulness of breathing, they really feel they are starting to get to the heart of meditation. In a way, they are right. My experience of teaching people mindfulness over many years, however, is that if I had started you straightaway with a full 20 minute mindfulness of breathing meditation, you would not have succeeded. Most people really do need to build up their powers of concentration slowly from a gentle start. And you have done that. Well done!

The full 20 minute mindfulness of breathing will really deepen your experience of meditation. I also find that this practice also helps people to become more mindful of their reactive thinking habits. Unhelpful thinking just can't help but keep popping up in the meditation itself. If this happens to you, just roll with it.

Notice your mind has wandered, and gently return to the practice.

After you have completed each meditation, give yourself a little reward, even if it is just a self-congratulatory pat on the back. Don't forget to give yourself a tick in the Progress Form.

At the end of the week, gather together all The Thinking Forms that you have collected from the beginning of the course. Use this opportunity to spend some time reflecting on the regular patterns that seem to crop up. Questions you might ask are:

Is there a dominant set of unhelpful reactive thinking habits I use regularly?
What kind of evidence do I habitually focus my attention on?
What kind of evidence do I habitually not look out for?
What have been my most effective strategies at countering my negative reactive thinking?

You are, of course, welcome to practice more than the five times suggested, but make sure you do manage the five times during the week.

If for any reason you have not managed the 5 meditations for this week, don't worry, sometimes life can get in the way, just start again from the beginning of Week 4. If this is the second consecutive week you haven't been able to stick to the routine, reflect on what has gone wrong, put remedies in place, and start again from Week 1.

If you have completed 5 meditations, well done, you're ready to move on to Week 5.

Week 5.

Complete your fifth TEDS self-assessment measure. Bear in mind how you have been feeling over the last week. Don't over analyze the questions. It is best to go with your gut reaction. Record your TEDS score in The Enlightenment Plan Progress Chart.

You are doing really well, we are almost at the half way point already!

This week we are increasing the amount of things to do by incorporating mindfulness practices too.

This week we have 3 aims:

1. Complete the Thought Form before and after every meditation, and
2. Start practicing the loving kindness meditation alternately with one other meditation of your choice, that's 5 meditations, each of 20 minutes length, and
3. Choose three mindfulness practices.

So in this week there is a lot that is new.

First, you have the chance to practice the loving kindness meditation for the first time. Follow the instruction in Chapter 7.

This is quite a different meditation, in that you will be using your imagination a great deal. For each of the people you need to bring to mind, you will have to imagine them in some way. Depending on your personal preferences, you can imagine them visually, in your mind's eye, or you can imagine hearing them. It's up to you. Experiment with what works best for you.

As you are new to the loving kindness meditation, remember to start with people you feel generally comfortable with. Ideally they should be about the same age as you, not a sexual partner, and the 'difficult person', should just be someone you have a mild difficulty with, not your archenemy.

This meditation does bring up some deep emotions for people from time to time, and not necessarily love or kindness. Whatever comes up for you, just accept it, and continue to intend good wishes to the people in your meditation.

The loving kindness meditation requires that you have a firm foundation in being able to concentrate. That is why I have introduced it now. It is also standard practice to alternative the loving kindness meditation with a more traditional focusing meditation. That is why I am asking you to alternate. It really is up to you whether you choose to do the Stress Buster or the mindfulness of breathing. If you are stressed or anxious right now, I would go with the Stress Buster meditation. If you are burdened by a mind pulling you in different directions, the mindfulness of breathing may be better for you. There are no rules, however, and finding your own rhythms is important. So feel free to experiment.

The second thing that is new is the mindfulness practice. Follow the instructions in Chapter 8. It really is up to you which mindfulness practices you start with. You only need to do three of the five I suggest. However, don't leave it to chance. Plan when you are going to do these practices as surely as if you were planning a meditation. Start by doing the easier practices first, like the mindful eating of a nut. You will be able to increase the complexity and/or length of the practice in the weeks to come.

When you start your mindfulness practice, try and bring the same kind of meditative awareness to the activity as you would in meditation itself. For most people it is easier to do this if you slow the activity down by at least half the normal speed.

You might choose to note down any experiences or insights you have for further reference.

So lots new this week. Remember, after you have completed each meditation and mindfulness exercise, give yourself a little reward, even if it is just a self-congratulatory pat on the back. Don't forget to give yourself a tick in the Progress Form after each meditation and mindfulness practice.

You are, of course, welcome to practice more than the five times suggested for the meditation, and three times for the mindfulness, but make sure you do manage the minimum amounts.

At the end of the week, collect Thinking Forms together, and try to find any patterns that keep cropping up. You might want to make a note of them.

If for any reason you have not managed 5 meditations and 3 mindfulness practices, don't worry; sometimes life can get in the way, just start again from the beginning of Week 5. If this is the second consecutive week you haven't been able to stick to the routine, reflect on what has gone wrong, put remedies in place, and start again from Week 1.

If you have completed 5 meditations and 3 mindfulness exercises, well done, you're ready to move onto Week 6.

Week 6.

Complete your sixth TEDS self-assessment measure. Bear in mind how you have been feeling over the last week. Don't over analyze the questions. It is best to go with your gut reaction. Record your TEDS score in The Enlightenment Plan Progress Chart.

Congratulations! You are now past the half way stage. Most people who get to this point finish the course and maintain meditation in their lives from now on. Given that you were stressed, anxious and/or depressed at the start of this program, that was some achievement. Give yourself a big 'high five'.

As you are half way through now, it is worth spending some time reflecting on the progress you have made. You have:

1. Learnt the Stress Buster meditation, and practiced it at least 100 minutes.
2. Learnt the mindfulness of breathing, and practiced it at least 150 minutes.
3. Learnt the loving kindness meditation and practiced it at least 60 minutes.
4. Done 40 minutes of further meditation of your choice.

   That's at least 350 minutes of meditation, or nearly 6 hours!

   Not only this,

5. You have learnt how to be mindful and challenge your reactive mind.

6. You have started to notice the patterns of your unhelpful thinking, and
7. You have started to develop your mindfulness skills, which, if you remember, are taking the skills of meditation into your daily life.

That is a lot! Well done!

Take some time now to reflect over the last five weeks, and write a list of all the things you have learnt, and all the progress you have made.

Do that now before moving on to My Promise:

My Promise: Your meditation practice will now start to bring you exponential benefit in the next five weeks. What do I mean by that? Well what I mean is that in the first five weeks, you will have gained about 25% of the benefit you will gain from The Enlightenment Plan. This means that as your practice deepens in the coming five weeks, the remaining 75% of the benefit of following The Enlightenment Plan is yet to come.

The reason I say this is that most of what you have achieved is simply laying the groundwork for what is yet to come. Remember I said learning meditation and CBT is a 'slow burn', that is to say, the benefits start small, and then suddenly 'catch fire'. Well it is about to get 'hot'. Are you excited? I hope so!

So let's move on. In Week 6, we have the following aims:

1. Complete the Thought Form before and after every meditation, and
2. Continue practicing the loving kindness meditation alternately with one other meditation of your choice, and

3. Choose three mindfulness practices.

This is essentially the same as the previous week. You might change which mindfulness practices you do, or deepen the ones you have already tried.

Just something extra you might try this week, at the end of the meditation and mindfulness practices; keep the mindful awareness going after the end of the formal practice. In other words, take your meditative sense of presence into your everyday life. See what happens. If it works for you, keep doing it in the weeks to come.

After you have completed each meditation and mindfulness task, give yourself a little reward, even if it is just a self-congratulatory pat on the back. Don't forget to give yourself a tick in the Progress Form after each meditation and mindfulness practice.

You are, of course, welcome to practice more than the five times suggested for the meditation and three times for the mindfulness, but make sure you do manage the minimum amounts.

At the end of the week, collect the Thinking Forms together, and try to find any patterns that keep cropping up. You might want to make a note of them.

If for any reason you have not managed 5 meditations and 3 mindfulness exercises, don't worry; sometimes life can get in the way, just start again from the beginning of Week 6. If this is the second consecutive week you haven't been able to stick to the routine, reflect on what has gone wrong, put remedies in place, and start again from Week 1.

If you have completed 5 meditations and 3 mindfulness exercises, well done, you're ready to move on to Week 7.

Week 7.

Complete your seventh TEDS self-assessment measure. Bear in mind how you have been feeling over the last week. Don't over analyze the questions. It is best to go with your gut reaction. Record your TEDS score in The Enlightenment Plan Progress Chart.

If you have got this far, I guess your meditation and mindfulness practice is going at least quite well. Lets face it, if you hated the practices you would have given up on them weeks ago. So I would like to congratulate you for getting this far, and invite you into the next stage.

This week we have three aims:

1. Complete the Thought Form before and after every meditation, and
2. Continue practicing in rotation all the 20 minute meditations learnt so far totaling at least 5 over the week, and
3. Choose four mindfulness practices.

Yes, we keep going with The Thought Forms; yes, we keep going with the meditations in free rotation; yes, we build and deepen the mindfulness practice. But this time I am going to share with you things I could have put in the introductory chapter but didn't. It would have simply sounded too weird and abstract. We are going to start talking in this week, and coming weeks, about 'presence'.

Unfortunately when we start getting to this level of our

understanding of meditation, words start to fail us. I'll tell you a story.

I remember, as a young boy, feeling part of the world but not part of the world, all at the same time. I tried to explain it to my older brother, but I couldn't find the words. His suggestion was if I didn't like the feeling, I shouldn't think about it. But this went far beyond mere thought, and anyway, I couldn't stop thinking about it.

The experience of being in the world, and not in the world, at the same time stayed with me. When I was 18 and was referred for therapy for my anxiety and depression, I tried to explain to the therapist what I experienced, but I was even worse at explaining to him what I was trying to communicate. It was as if there was something about the world, something about its very essence, or 'suchness', that I couldn't quite put into words.

I suppose the mystery of my experience continued, because it motivated much of my academic work. The nearest solution to this conundrum I could find was in the social philosophy of Alfred Schutz (1899-1959). He suggested that for all practical purposes, people ignore the 'suchness' of the world (to use my phrase) and work on the basis that we share the same world in common.

In a way this solved only half of the problem, the problem of 'intersubjectivity'. Schutz suggested we simply proceed on the basis that we share in common the same world. But what of my world of 'suchness', the world that I was struggling to express?

I suppose this world only started to make sense when I began meditating and became acquainted with the philosophies of the

East. There I found my problem encapsulated in words for the first time. Here is Lau Tzu's famous quote which describes it perfectly:

"The Tao that can be said, is not the eternal Tao":

I didn't feel quite so mad after all. Other people had struggled with the same things I had struggled with. The 'eternal Tao' is something other people have peered into too, and found it just as indescribable.

Now of course the thing that doesn't matter here is the Tao, it is just a name for ultimate reality, so I don't want to go down that route. I simply want to notice that other people have had experiences of their world that defy description.

'Presence' is one of those words. And if you were thinking this doesn't apply to you, then you are mistaken. You have been meditating now for six weeks, this is the seventh. My strong suspicion is that you have already started to experience 'presence', but have just not realized what it is, and its significance for you.

'Presence' is those times in meditation when the discursive, reactive mind is simply silent.

I appreciate that these moments don't happen very often, and when they do, they don't last very long. It's the same for me. But if you have got this far, they will almost certainly occasionally be happening.

So this week, continue the practice as usual, but look out for those moments when your mind, your conscious automatic thinking, falls silent. That is presence. Pay attention, and allow the presence to be there. If you do, you will be well positioned to take the next step, but that doesn't happen until next week.

Beware! Please don't flick through to next week. This cannot be understood intellectually. It is not of the mind, it stands outside the mind, and that is the only clue I will give you.

Just allow yourself to be present to 'presence'.

After you have completed each meditation and mindfulness exercise, give yourself a little reward, even if it is just a self-congratulatory pat on the back. Don't forget to give yourself a tick in the Progress Form after each meditation and mindfulness exercise.

You are, of course, welcome to practice more than the five times suggested for the meditation and the four times for the mindfulness. In fact this is a good time to start going over the minimum if you can find the time. But do make sure you manage the five meditations and four mindfulness exercises as a minimum during the week.

At the end of the week, collect your Thinking Forms together, and try to find any patterns that keep cropping up. You might want to make a note of them.

If for any reason you have not managed 5 meditations and 4 mindfulness exercises, don't worry; sometimes life can get in the way, just start again from the beginning of Week 7. If this is the second consecutive week you haven't been able to stick to the routine, reflect on what has gone wrong, put remedies in place, and start again from Week 1.

If you have completed 5 meditations and 4 mindfulness exercises, well done, you're ready to move on to Week 8.

Week 8.

Complete your eighth TEDS self-assessment measure. Bear in mind how you have been feeling over the last week. Don't over analyze the questions. It is best to go with your gut reaction. Record your TEDS score in The Enlightenment Plan Progress Chart.

Our aims for this week are:

1. Complete the Thought Form before and after every meditation, and
2. Continue practicing in rotation all the meditations learnt so far, and
3. Choose four mindfulness practices, and
4. Reflect on, 'Am I my thoughts'?

Last week I invited you to be present to 'presence', the place you go in meditation when the reactive mind stops. I understand it is difficult, and those moments don't last long, but I hope you agree, they are there.

So we have something of a mystery. We have two ways of being in meditation.

1. The Tao that can be said, or in our terms, the chatter of the conscious mind, and
2. The Tao that cannot be said, or in our terms, the times when you are present to being 'present', without the chatter of the conscious mind.

So this week, yes I want you to continue all the practices we have been describing, but also continue to pay attention to those moments that go beyond words. The moments you are simply 'present' to the 'suchness' of things.

You might further reflect, if the thoughts can quieten and still, and 'I' am still there, are you your thoughts, or are you something other than your thoughts?

After you have completed each meditation, give yourself a little reward, even if it is just a self-congratulatory pat on the back. Don't forget to give yourself a tick in the Progress Form.

You are, of course, welcome to practice more than the five times suggested, but make sure you do manage the five times during the week.

At the end of the week, collect Thinking Forms together, and try to find any patterns that keep cropping up. You might want to make a note of them.

If for any reason you have not managed 5 meditations and four mindfulness practices, don't worry, sometimes life can get in the way, just start again from the beginning of Week 8. If this is the second consecutive week you haven't been able to stick to the routine, reflect on what has gone wrong, put remedies in place, and start again from Week 1.

If you have completed 5 meditations and 4 mindfulness practices, well done, you're ready to move onto Week 9.

Week 9.

Complete your ninth TEDS self-assessment measure. Bear in mind how you have been feeling over the last week. Don't over analyze the questions. It is best to go with your gut reaction. Record your TEDS score in The Enlightenment Plan Progress Chart.

This week, we have four aims:

1. Complete the Thought Form before and after every meditation, and
2. Practice The Enlightenment Meditation alternately with any other practice, and
3. Complete all five mindfulness practices, and
4. Reflect on "Can stress, anxiety and depression remain if you are present to it"?

Over the last two weeks, in addition to the practices, I have been inviting you to focus in on those moments when thought recedes, and you are left simply being present to what is.

This week, we turbo charge that experience with The Enlightenment Meditation. Here, after we have settled the body, the breath and the mind, we simply rest in 'presence' and wait for the mind to start up. In this frame of mind, you are literally practicing 'being' enlightened.

Of course, these moments won't last long, so be kind to yourself when your discursive reactive mind objects and starts throwing thoughts at you. You may be being enlightened for just a few seconds, but it's a start! This is a seed that will grow to full irreversible enlightenment.

So again, deepen your awareness of presence. This week, my question for you is 'Is it possible for stress, anxiety and depression to remain if you are present'? You will get my thoughts on this next week, so please don't take a peek. This is much more effective if you work it out for yourself. Try it for yourself.

After you have completed each meditation and mindfulness practice, give yourself a little reward, even if it is just a self-congratulatory pat on the back. Don't forget to give yourself a tick in the Progress Form after each meditation and mindfulness practice.

You are, of course, welcome to practice more than the five times suggested for meditation and mindfulness, but make sure you do manage the five times for both during the week.

At the end of the week, collect the Thinking Forms together, and try to find any patterns that keep cropping up. You might want to make a note of them.

If for any reason you have not managed 5 meditations, don't worry; sometimes life can get in the way, just start again from the beginning of Week 9. If this is the second consecutive week you haven't been able to stick to the routine, reflect on what has gone wrong, put remedies in place, and start again from Week 1.

If you have completed 5 meditations and mindfulness practices, well done: you're ready to move onto Week 10.

Week 10.

Complete your tenth TEDS self-assessment measure. Bear in mind how you have been feeling over the last week. Don't over analyze the questions. It is best to go with your gut reaction. Record your TEDS score in The Enlightenment Plan Progress Chart.

We are nearly at the end. Congratulations, nearly there!

Here are the aims for this week:

1. Complete the Thought Form before and after every meditation, and
2. Practice The Enlightenment Meditation alternately with any other practice, and
3. Complete all five mindfulness practices, and
4. Try "being present "to emotional pain.

So, can stress, anxiety and depression remain if you are present, which is to say, your discursive reactive mind subsides? I hope you discovered the answer for yourself? Here's my take.

Well there are two answers to this. The first is to make the unremarkable observation that when we are 'present' to our experience, time itself seems to disappear. Now this, of course, isn't suggesting that in some ultimate sense, time disappears, just our experience of time disappears.

As you are now aware, for stress, anxiety and depression to be present in our experience, we are caught up with ruminating about what has happened or what is about to happen. In other words stress anxiety and depression need our awareness of time to exist. If we are present, and our awareness of time fades, so must our stressed, anxious and depressed thoughts.

So I hope you discovered the same. When you were present, your stressed, anxious and depressed thinking also faded, if only for a moment.

The second answer is that your stressed, anxious or depressed thoughts may fade, but you might still be aware of the emotional pain in your body.

My suggestion is, just as in Chapter 9, if you bring your presence, that is to say, your present conscious awareness into the pain, allow the pain to be there with non-judgmental kindness, and the pain simply cannot help but dissolve over time.

If you don't believe it ... just try it and see for yourself. In fact, this is my final suggestion for you on this course.

Try it, and you will find that meditation and mindfulness will heal your life.

After you have completed each meditation and mindfulness practice, give yourself a little reward, even if it is just a self-congratulatory pat on the back. Don't forget to give yourself a tick in the Progress Form after each meditation and mindfulness practice.

Complete a final TEDS questionnaire and reflect on the progression of the scores from week 1. Also collect the Thinking Forms together, and try to find any patterns that keep cropping up. You might want to make a note of them.

If for any reason you have not managed 5 meditations, don't worry, sometimes life can get in the way, just start again from the beginning of Week 10.

The End:

So that's it.

You have done really well to get through the 10 weeks. I genuinely hope The Enlightenment Plan has helped to move your life in a more positive direction.
Now is a good time to go through all The Thinking forms you have collected over the last 10 weeks. I imagine they tell quite a journey.

Also retake for one last time the TEDS and plot a graph showing your progress.

Top Tip: Take this opportunity to reflect and list everything you have learnt, and devise a plan for how you need to move your life forward.

You have learnt the essence of western psychology, and the essence of eastern mysticism. You now have everything you need to continue to transform your life positively. These ten weeks, I hope, have been just the start. Continue with the practices, and they will continue to subtly transform and heal your life. They have the power, in fact, to end all suffering, to take you to enlightenment itself.

www.ingramcontent.com/pod-product-compliance
Lightning Source LLC
Chambersburg PA
CBHW060104230426
43661CB00033B/1415/J